WHOSE VALUES?

Whose Values?

*The Battle for Morality in
Pluralistic America*

Edited by Carl Horn

SERVANT BOOKS
Ann Arbor, Michigan

Available from Servant Books, Box 8617, Ann Arbor,
    Michigan 48107.

ISBN 0-89283-180-4

Printed in the United States of America
85 86 87 88   10 9 8 7 6 5 4 3 2 1

**Library of Congress Cataloging in Publication Data
    Main entry under title:**

Whose values?

1. United States—Religion—1960   —Addresses,
essays, lectures.   2. United States—Moral conditions
—Addresses, essays, lectures.   3. Religion and
state—United States—History—20th century—
Addresses, essays, lectures.   4. Religious pluralism—
Addresses, essays, lectures.   I. Horn, Carl.
BL2525.W48 1985   261.1'0973   84-19339
ISBN 0-89283-180-4

Contents

Contributors / vii

Introduction / 1

1. The Politics of Morality and Religion:
   A Primer / 5
   Terry Eastland

2. Disentangling the Secular Humanism
   Debate / 21
   James Hitchcock

3. "Secular Humanism" or "The American
   Way" / 37
   Joseph Sobran

4. On Parents, Children, and the Nation-State / 53
   Allan C. Carlson

5. Abortion: the Judeo-Christian Imperative / 73
   W. Douglas Badger

6. Rationalizing Infanticide: Medical Ethics in the
   Eighties / 95
   James Manney

7. Ideological Biases in Today's Theories of Moral
   Education / 113
   Paul Vitz

8. Trends in State Regulation of Religious
   Schools / 139
   William B. Ball

9. Pluralism and the Limits of Neutrality / 153
   Francis Canavan, S.J.

10. "World Views" and Public Policy / 167
    Carl Horn

Notes / 187

Contributors

W. Douglas Badger is legislative director for the Christian Action Council.

William B. Ball is a partner in the law firm of Ball and Skelly, Harrisburg, Pennsylvania. He has argued seven major religious freedom cases before the U.S. Supreme Court.

Rev. Francis Canavan, S.J. is professor of political science at Fordham University.

Allan C. Carlson is executive vice president of the Rockford Institute.

Terry Eastland is special assistant to the U.S. Attorney General. Formerly editor of the Norfolk *Virginian Pilot*, he is co-author of *Counting by Race: Equality from the Founding Fathers to Bakke and Weber*.

James Hitchcock is professor of history at St. Louis University. His books include *Catholicism and Modernity*, *The Recovery of the Sacred*, and *What Is Secular Humanism?*

Carl Horn is president of the North Carolina Policy Council. He has been special assistant to the Assistant Attorney General for Civil Rights and general counsel of the Christian Legal Society.

James Manney is a senior editor at Servant Publications. He is co-author (with John C. Blattner) of *Death in the Nursery: The Secret Crime of Infanticide*.

Joseph Sobran is a nationally syndicated columnist and radio commentator. An editor of *National Review*, he is author of *Single Issues*.

Paul Vitz is associate professor of psychology at New York University. His books include *Psychology as Religion: The Myth of Self-Worship*.

WHOSE VALUES?

Introduction

WHOSE BELIEFS AND VALUES should form the basis for legal and public policy decisions in our pluralistic society? What "world-view"—whose moral vision—ought to be taught in our public schools? How do we determine what behavior will be left to private choice, and which will be deemed "illegal?" Is it wrong to prohibit homosexual "couples" from adopting children? Whose values do we favor where there are differences of opinion in the body politic over questions such as these?

Much argument is currently being made for and against the proposition that America was, and is, a Christian nation. This book of essays avoids that debate because, irrespective of its outcome, it is clear that the foundation of our public moral judgments has historically been the Judeo-Christian ethic. That is not to say that the argument over Christian America is nonconsequential or unimportant, but rather that traditional moral and family-centered values can be defended without having to prove this harder case. This being true, we opt for the easier proof.

Many public issues have surfaced in recent years which illustrate an underlying conflict in fundamental values, or "world-views," among the American populace: abortion; infanticide (intentional starvation or medical nontreatment of less-than-perfect newborns); state regulation and harassment of religious schools; public funding of Planned Parenthood; distribution of birth control prescriptions and devices to minor girls without parental notification or consent; proliferation of pornography, including child pornography; prosecution of parents who choose to educate their children in unlicensed church schools or at home; increasingly strident demands to expand homosexual rights and influence; and arguments for the "strict separation" of church and state.

Together, these and related controversies point to a deeper and more fundamental "values crisis" in contemporary American life. Again, the persistent question is *whose* beliefs and values should be reflected in the law and public policy of our pluralistic society. This is, by any account, a complex question—which makes it all the more regrettable that most of what we hear and read in the popular media is so superficial and results-oriented in nature.

We are often told, for example, that Judeo-Christian beliefs and values cannot be reflected in our law or public policy because this would "impose" or "legislate" morality and would violate "the separation of church and state," a fundamental tenet of our "pluralism." There are instances where this is true, of course, but when stated as a blanket principle, without caveat or qualification, it becomes little more than a misleading half-truth.

This book of essays suggests four propositions in rebuttal to the assertion that Judeo-Christian ethics and values must be excluded from our public life and decisions. Briefly stated, they are; (1) again and again, the question is not *whether* values are going to be imposed or legislated, but *whose* values; (2) we may be a pluralistic society, but we are not a radically secular society; (3) the separation of *church* and state does not mean or require the separation of *religion* and state, or worse, the separation of *traditional values* and state; and (4) the controversial social questions of the day (abortion and school prayer, for example) are best understood, not as conservative efforts to impose or legislate, but as a conservative or traditional response to relatively recent assaults on established morals and principles.

For far too long Christians, Jews, and others who subscribe to traditional moral values have allowed the illogical and ahistorical arguments of radical secularism to go unchallenged. As a result, value-laden decisions and programs which contradict and compete with traditional Judeo-Christian beliefs and values have become increasingly entrenched. "Values neutrality" and "pluralism" have, in effect, become little more than code words used in the service of a secularist moral and ethical perspective of man and society. That this is hardly "values neutral" has frequently and conveniently gone unnoticed.

But the balance of power is shifting, both intellectually and politically. Secular liberalism no longer commands the respect it once did and those who hold to traditional moral and ethical values are clearly on the ascendancy. Aleksandr Solzhenitsyn's criticism of Western society as suffering "the flaw of a consciousness lacking all divine dimension" has really hit home. Americans remain a deeply religious people, and this deeper vein of our heritage is being mined with increasing sophistication and effectiveness.

The essays in this book are representative of this swing of the sacred-secular pendulum in the direction of the reaffirmation of traditional moral and family-centered values. The authors, a number of whom hold Ph.D.'s from major universities, are not reactionaries or obscurantists. Although the collective view is clearly sympathetic to a broader role for traditional religious and moral values, the analysis and argument in this collection of essays is fresh, vital, and creative. All who sincerely seek a satisfactory societal resolution of the current values crisis—and that is precisely what it is—will benefit from a careful reading and consideration of the points they raise. The alternative is sociological, and spiritual, disaster.

The ancient Hebrew scripture emphasizes the importance that any people have on informing and motivating "vision." "Where there is no vision," teaches one of the Hebrew proverbs, "the people perish," or "are unrestrained," according to a second translation. Modern American society is certainly testimony to the truth of this ancient proverb (Prv

29:18), and the current social disharmony and conflict can only be expected to increase until the questions raised in these essays are sensitively and satisfactorily addressed.

Whose beliefs and values will we affirm in our public institutions and decisions? What are the requirements—and the limits—of our pluralism? What core values will we affirm in order to hold our pluralistic society together? In short, to use the biblical term, what is our *vision* for the America of the 1980s, the 1990s, and beyond? These are the questions which the reader should keep in mind while enjoying and pondering the essays in this book.

CARL HORN

ONE

The Politics of Morality and Religion: a Primer

Terry Eastland

FOR MANY YEARS it was common to refer to our nation as a Christian nation, not in any particular denominational sense, but generally, broadly, "merely Christian," to adapt a term from C.S. Lewis. Politicians said so, teachers said so, even some judges said so; and so did Americans from all walks of life. And indeed they did so justifiably, for America was a Christian nation.

Today, however, this can no longer be said with much confidence. America is in a period of transition, from a Christian nation to a secular one.

Two trends are telling. One is that over the past two decades the public schools have been formally rid of all religious influences except "objective" teaching about religion. The only prayer sure to pass constitutional muster today is the one said silently, presumably as the teacher hands out the final exams. Devotional exercises are out, and not even a copy of one of the most significant religious and moral documents in the history of the West—the Ten Commandments—may be posted by the state in a public school classroom.

The other trend is that morality today is increasingly viewed as a matter of who decides, rather than what is decided. That is, the act of choosing, rather than what is chosen, has become for many the decisive ethical issue. Inevitably, the focus on individual choice has diminished the influence of families and communities and the substantive moralities they historically have endorsed through law and ordinance. In 1973 the Supreme Court ratified and strengthened this trend by announcing a mother's right to seek an abortion, thus vacating the fifty state laws on abortion, all of which reflected judgments about the morality of abortion.

Some Christians are equanimous about these trends; indeed, some are so approving as to suggest that private religion—a religion with little or no public influence—is fine by them. After all, they contend, students can still pray silently in school, can't they? And mothers can still draw on personal religious beliefs in deciding about abortion, can they not? But other Christians are deeply disturbed by the situation today. And when they speak out, they frequently find themselves on the defensive. They are told that their views on church and state mix the two institutions in violation of the Constitution, Supreme Court edict, sound public policy, and American history. This is heavy artillery to have to receive, yet to their credit these Christians have persevered, insisting that something has gone seriously wrong with our nation and that something must be done to recover our heritage—our Christian heritage.

This article is written for the Christian who finds himself to one degree or another in this position. It is an attempt to provide the Christian, not with a legislative or policy agenda, but with a general understanding of the relationship of politics and religion in America. Accordingly, this is an essay about ideas—about natural rights, separation of church and state, federalism, and virtue, among others. And to understand these ideas, it is necessary to approach them in historical context.

This essay—this primer on politics—is, necessarily, devoted in large part to the American founding.

At its birth as a nation America was a remarkable union of Enlightenment ideas and Protestant culture. Enlightenment ideas provided much of the intellectual framework for the American republic. The Protestant Christianity of the Colonies also contributed to that framework, but more importantly it nourished the kind of citizens democracies presuppose. Two centuries later we see that tensions can arise between Enlightenment thought and Christian faith. But at the American founding these tensions had yet to develop.

The history of political philosophy in the West can be divided into two eras—the one before Thomas Hobbes, the Englishman who lived from 1588 to 1697, and the one after Hobbes. Hobbes rejected the ancient tradition of political philosophy which held that man reaches the perfection of his nature only in and through civil society. In this tradition, civil society—political society—was prior to the individual, and the duties were prior to rights—rights, in fact, were almost nonexistent. In rejecting this tradition, Hobbes specifically denied that the state exists to make men better. The state, in his view, cannot exist for this purpose, because the state cannot presume to know what is best for man. Inasmuch as priests and clerics had played large roles in determining how the state should govern, Hobbes sought to diminish their influence. Indeed, he sought to exclude it altogether.

Hobbes maintained that instead of starting with the state, political science should begin with man as he is, an individual existing in a state of nature apart from civil society. In this state—a theoretical condition—each man has the natural right to preserve himself. Hobbes left determination of the proper means for exercising this right to the individual, not to men of presumed superior wisdom—such as, in his view, men of the cloth. For Hobbes it followed that an individual could do whatever his self-preservation required—everything would be a legitimate means to this end.

Hobbes further taught that men could consent to the creation of a sovereign whose job would be that of keeping the peace. The critical word in this teaching is "consent." Men had to consent, or else the sovereign could not legitimately rule. The state thus had no existence apart from man—there was no divine right of kings. Instead, man was the source of all political authority—man was the measure of all political things.

According to Hobbes, justice is a matter of fulfilling the obligations that derive from consent—from contract. As Leo Strauss wrote of Hobbes' teaching, "All material obligations arise from the agreement of the contractors, and therefore in practice from the will of the sovereign." The contract making possible all other contracts, for Hobbes, was, as Strauss said, "the social contract . . . to the sovereign."

Hobbes was without question one of the most important political thinkers of the Enlightenment. His ideas, transmitted and developed through successive generations of thinkers, especially John Locke, deeply influenced the birth of America as a nation. Thanks in large part to the Enlightenment, America is a natural rights regime. And thanks in large part to the Enlightenment, America has a separate church and state.

Yet the America that owes much to the Enlightenment did not accept its political teachings without qualification. In regard to natural rights, Americans did not generally make the argument for natural rights as Hobbes, for example, made it and as in fact it can be made—independent of God. The Declaration of Independence maintained that men are "endowed by their Creator with certain unalienable Rights." That was written, of course, by Thomas Jefferson, hardly a traditional Christian, but the Declaration, as Jefferson said, reflected the common sense at the time. And it was common at that time to believe both in natural rights and that God endowed man with these rights.

The clergy preached on natural rights—arguing for their existence as given by God. And this position was natural to the kind of religion developing since the first settlements in America in the early seventeenth century. This religion was Christian, specifically Protestant, more specifically radical (for the time) Protestant. It taught salvation by faith and the priesthood of all believers; it focused on the individual and his individual conversion. It also taught the idea of covenant, which is closely related to the political idea of consent. The Protestant Christianity of early America thus was naturally disposed not only toward natural rights, when qualified as God given, but also toward the arguments flowing from natural rights—that the purpose of government, as the Declaration of Independence stated, is to secure rights; and that all government requires the consent of the governed.

In regard to separation of church and state, it is true that some Americans—most noticeably Jefferson and Madison— seemed at times almost Hobbesian in spirit. Like Hobbes, these Americans tended to see religion as a divisive force. They tended to agree with Montesquieu who had written that even in its coolest state "religion has been much oftener a motive to oppression than a restraint from it." The urgency for these Americans, as for Hobbes, was to separate church and state by as much distance as possible—on occasion these Americans seemed to want to exclude from public life the influence of religion altogether.

But not all Americans viewed religion as Jefferson and Madison did. Indeed, it is probable that only a minority— admittedly an influential minority—saw religion this way. Americans generally were positively disposed towards religion, and of course by "religion" they meant the religion of the Colonies—the Christian religion. And they saw the issue of church and state primarily in terms of religious freedom, for both theological and practical reasons.

The Protestant focus on the individual believer emphasized the importance of his response to God; religious liberty thus was regarded as an essential condition of the act of faith. Furthermore, America was home to more "sects" or denominations than any other nation. There were not only Episcopalians and Congregationalists but also Presbyterians, Methodists, Baptists, Quakers, and still others. Moreover, America seemed a natural place for churches to split and splinter—witness the "Old Lights" and the "New Lights" in mid-eighteenth-century New England. The Protestant variety—and the tendency towards still greater variety—thus required the elbow room provided by religious liberty. Not surprisingly, most Christians came to perceive a state church as a threat to religious liberty.

By the latter quarter of the eighteenth century, a consensus had developed regarding religion and politics. Americans were generally against state establishment or preferential treatment of a particular church or creed. Yet they were generally supportive of religion—meaning, of course, the Christian religion. This consensus lay behind the Constitution written in Philadelphia in 1787 and the First Amendment, which was added in 1791.

The framers of that document gave Congress no power to create a state church. And in its only reference to religion, the Constitution explicitly forbade the requirement of any "religious test" as a "qualification to any office or public trust under the United States."

When five states and a portion of a sixth wanted an explicit guarantee against a single national religious establishment and in favor of the rights of conscience, the text that became our First Amendment was written by the First Congress. Ratified by the states in 1791, the amendment says, in relevant part, "Congress shall make no law respecting an establishment of religion, or prohibiting the free exercise thereof."

Applied to the national government, specifically to the Congress, the amendment was a guarantee both to the states and to individual citizens; it was a protection for both, against certain action by the national government. From what is known of the debates in the First Congress, it is apparent that the framers intended to bar Congress from setting up a national church or according any preferred legal status to a church.

Beyond this, however, the framers did not go. There seems to be no evidence that they desired to preclude federal aid to churches or religions so long as the aid furthered a public purpose and was provided on a basis that did not discriminate among them. Neither is there evidence to indicate they wished to end all government involvements in religion.

Moreover, actions of the same Congress that framed the First Amendment indicate a general acceptance of various kinds of church-and-state involvements. This Congress retained chaplains and provided for a military chaplain. It called for a proclamation for a day of prayer and thanksgiving to God that President Washington subsequently issued. It also re-enacted the Northwest Ordinance, first passed in 1787, which declared: "Religion, morality and knowledge, being necessary to good government and the happiness of mankind, schools and the means of education shall forever be encouraged."

The nature of the original Constitution, the meaning of the First Amendment, and the national involvements with religion reflected the consensus on religion and politics at the American founding. As Justice Story later pointed out, it was "the general, if not the universal, sentiment in America . . . that Christianity ought to receive encouragement from the State." And this encouragement, of course, did not include establishment or preferential treatment of a church or creed.

Frequently, in discussing politics and religion at the American founding, the states are neglected. But they should not be. The Constitution was written in such a way that power was divided between the national government and the states. And generally speaking, the founders' "federalism" left to the states decisions regarding religion and morality.

In the final decades of the eighteenth century and the first decades of the nineteenth, two trends were evident in the states in regard to religion. On the one hand, the states with established churches in the states disestablished them. By

1776, the Anglican establishments in Maryland, South Carolina, North Carolina, and Georgia had been toppled. In 1802 Virginia's Anglican establishment, considerably weakened during the founding period, was ended. In 1833 the final establishment from colonial days—the Congregational Church in Massachusetts—was quietly eliminated.

On the other hand, the states acted in support of the Christian faith. Thus, state constitutional and statutory provisions declared it to be "the duty of all men to worship the Supreme Being, the Great Creator and Preserver of the Universe." The states regulated membership in Christian denominations. The states imposed fines for failure to attend worship services on the Lord's day. The states required elected officials to swear that they "believe the Christian religion, and have a firm persuasion of its truth." And the states established public education for the purpose—recalling the language of the Northwest Ordinance—of promoting "religion, morality and knowledge."

These trends in the states perfectly reflected the consensus on politics and religion at the American founding. And it is in the state actions in support of religion that the Christian character of early America can be clearly seen—more clearly, in fact, than in the federal actions. Most Americans were Christian—if not actively so, certainly in a cultural sense. And this social reality had political relevance extending far beyond the various state actions.

The fact of the matter is, Christianity filled a seldom-noticed vacuum in the political science of the founding fathers. This vacuum may be described as moral, which is not to say the founders were unethical. The founders were engaged in a novel enterprise of nation-building, and they were aware of the trade-offs and difficulties of the choices they faced; there was, as they well knew, no perfect political arrangement. They were not utopians, but realists. In siding with the modern political philosophers, and against the ancients, they decided to take man as he was—not as he can be. And in striving to protect his liberties, they found they could not also attempt to make him virtuous.

Even so, the founders could not entirely dismiss the question of virtue. They believed that some degree of virtue in the people would be necessary if America were to endure as a free nation. As James Madison said at the Virginia Ratifying Convention, "to suppose that any form of government will secure liberty or happiness without any virtue in the people is a chimerical idea." The founders, however, plead for virtue to a far greater extent than they provided institutionally for it. And it is fair to say that they were lucky. They were born at the right time for launching the American experiment in self-government. For eighteenth-century America was home to a people of the right virtues, the "right stuff"—a people fit for democracy.

To be sure, the civilization in North America during the American founding was human and afflicted with the ills of the human condition—greed, pettiness, selfishness, and the rest. But the civilization also was nurtured by classical and especially Christian traditions—pre-modern traditions. And these traditions—especially Christianity—supplied what the political science of the founding did not—and could not. It was the institution that inculcated in Americans the virtues needed for self-government.

During the seventeenth and eighteenth centuries Americans were nurtured on a faith that was Reformed in theology, Puritan in outlook, experiential in faith, and evangelical toward the world. Almost every denomination—Anglican, Presbyterian, Congregational, Methodist, Baptist—was influenced heavily by the Westminster Confession of 1643. The prevailing religion was one of the book—the Bible.

The Protestant Reformation reformed what the mass of people did with their eyes. For it was only after the Reformation that men of all stations in life began to read. And what they read was the Bible. In seventeenth- and eighteenth-century America, learning to read was a devotional exercise.

Children learned their ABC's from hornbooks and then the New England Primer, both of which were didactic introductions to reading. The hornbooks, for example, typically included not only the alphabet but also the Lord's prayer, a benediction, and a brief religious admonition. Children read the Bible and various spiritual guides and testimonial works, all of which sought to inculcate Christian character.

According to Lawrence Cremin, the five most popular books during America's first 150 years were religious books—John Foxe's *Acts and Monuments*; Lewis Bayly's *The Practise of Pietie*; Richard Allestree's *TheWhole Duty of Man*; Richard Baxter's *The Poor Man's Family Book*; and John Bunyan's *The Pilgrim's Progress*. These books constituted the educational philosophy of the colonies. Their source was the Bible, their voice sermonic, their method of instruction casuistry—the application of religious and moral principles to particular situations. Adults read these books, and the educational philosophy they contained—the practice of true piety—influenced the rearing of children. Indeed the books explicitly instructed readers to educate their children in Christian faith. In *Pilgrim's Progress,* for example, Dame Mercy catechizes Christian's children to see whether they have been properly instructed in the faith.

Protestant Christianity thus tutored the first generations of Americans. It provided what we today would call the value system of the society. it is, of course, true that many early Americans did not go regularly to church; many were nominal Christians. But even these Americans tended to be well acquainted with the Bible and the fundamentals of Christian faith. Most Americans had a common frame of reference, and, whatever the degree of belief on the part of each individual, this frame of reference was deeply influenced by Christianity.

For example, Americans generally agreed with John Adams that our laws—both constitutional and statutory—were rooted in a common moral and religious tradition. This tradition went back as far as Mount Sinai, where Moses received the Ten Commandments. Americans thus had a high view of law. It was not simply the creation of man, and it was not to be treated lightly. Law, moreover, was seen as a pointer or witness to the collective fulfillment of a higher aspiration and destiny. It was the expression of a people whose ancestors came to America in order to build a better social order than the one they left.

Christianity provided an attitude toward law that law itself could not provide. It instilled in Americans the civic virtues of respect for legitimate authority and obedience to it. By strengthening the legal order, Christianity in turn strengthened the social order and thus the bonds of community from which emerge still other civic virtues—those of altruism, neighborliness, and patriotism.

Christianity influenced individual and community behavior. Although Americans had considerable freedoms, their religion, as Tocqueville observed, prevented them from even contemplating certain courses of action, and forbade them to dare taking them. Christianity generally constrained the society; it made firm the distinction between the responsible exercise of liberty, and license.

Christianity specifically taught, in addition to the spiritual virtues, those of sobriety, honesty, prudence, temperance, and diligence. In the context of these virtues, as Irving Kristol has pointed out, capitalism made ethical sense. Protestantism was understood to tame and direct a man's interests, including his economic ones, to higher ends. Christianity taught that man was a steward upon earth, and that he was to use his liberty and his talents responsibly (and not slothfully). The Larger Catechism of the Westminster Confession, which one writer called the "reigning theology of the country," taught early Americans a variety of duties that bear on the conduct of commercial life. These included "truth, faithfulness, and justice in contracts and commerce"; "moderation of our judgments, wills, and affections, concerning worldly goods"; "a lawful calling, and diligence in it"; "frugality"; and "avoiding unnecessary lawsuits."

The long and short of it is that during its first 200 years, America was a Christian nation. Christianity nourished the first generations of Americans. It set individual and community standards. It supplied the virtues a nation conceived in liberty would need. It answered the oldest of political questions—that of the kind of people a society produces.

This, then, was America at its birth—a product not only of the Enlightenment but also Protestant Christianity. If America was an impossibility before the Enlightenment, it was equally an impossibility before the Protestant Revolution. This peculiar nation was not explicitly Christian—in the sense of a Constitution that declares fidelity to Christian faith. But it was in its guts Christian, for Christianity shaped the society and the individuals who lived in it.

Today, much has changed. The culture is not discernibly Christian, and neither is the nation, at least not in its public life.

In terms of ideas, it is fair to describe this change by saying that the Enlightenment has scored significant victories against the Christian culture which long ago accepted it. The plant has taken over much of the garden, and made it a different place.

Natural rights are no longer seen by the most influential Americans as God given. Neither are they generally deemed as inherent in nature. Few people today speak of natural rights, but, simply, rights. And rights are lawyer- and judge-given, things to be created as circumstances require. And it would appear that there have been plenty of such circumstances—a culture insistent on rights and necessarily focused on the individual has developed. Here perhaps the most significant indication of change is the 1973 abortion decision, which asserted the right to an abortion, largely leaving to the mother the issue of deciding the fate of her unborn.

In this culture of rights, religion is permitted, but only so long as it has little or no public dimension—which is to say, only so long as the individual keeps it to himself. The principle of separating church and state, which at the founding only separated the national government from a church, has been used, among other things, to separate public education from significant religious influence. The Hobbesian hostility toward religion that some founding fathers seemed to share has become an article of faith for many who eagerly support a much higher wall of separation of church and state than the consensus at the founding intended. Editorials insistent on keeping high the "wall" between church and state almost invariably refer to the "divisive" nature of religion. Montesquieu is not out of date: religion is regarded by many today as a "motive for oppression." Religion may be all right, but only if it is kept in the right place, within the individual's bosom.

The triumph of the Enlightenment is not complete; the movement to a culture of rights in which the public influence of religion is minimized is unfinished. But more movement in this direction is possible; there are plaintiffs in court every day, and the possibilities for the creation of more rights and the further privatization of religion are strong indeed. The triumph of the Enlightenment will be upon us when we are so awash in rights that we are virtually unable to pass legislation reflecting traditional religious and moral views. Moral relativism then will be the rule, at law; and what is true at law will shape what is practiced. For when morality is strictly up to the individual, with no judgment possible by communities, it is likely that everyone will do what is right in his own eyes, as was true long ago in Canaan, during the reign of the Judges. America will then become a land composed of strangers whose religion, if any, is a private matter, and who are bound by no social ties or common aspirations.

If this point is reached, there will be little if any collective moral strength left in the nation. And the implications of this circumstance go beyond issues of education and community morality. For our very ability to defend ourselves as a nation will be in doubt, and our vulnerability to saviors both foreign and domestic will be conspicuous. In short, the day will have arrived when the prospect for the American future is gravely in doubt.

Christians concerned about the condition of our country are right to be concerned. An intellectual may say that the triumph of the Enlightenment is inevitable. He may say, that is, that Christianity lost when Hobbes changed the course of political philosophy by arguing for natural rights and seeking to minimize the influence of the clergy upon politics. But the Christian cannot accept arguments of inevitability. Christianity is a faith of possibility, of hope and change. It is the most dynamic social force in the history of Western civilization. America itself is testimony to its force.

What is the Christian to do? To begin with, he would be well advised to understand the political arrangements put in place by the Founding Fathers, and to seek their renewal today. Christians know that no political system can be perfect. Systems can only be better or worse, but the system established 200 years ago was not bad at all. The problem today is not with the system but with what has happened to it.

The founding fathers regarded the third branch of government—the judicial branch—as "the least dangerous." Its role was limited in the sense that the courts were not to make policy—that was the job of the legislature. But increasingly over the past 100 years, the federal judiciary has made more and more policy, expanding its role far beyond what the framers intended. Much of this policy-making expansion has occurred through the judiciary's willingness to extend the guarantees of the Bill of Rights, which originally applied only to the national government, to the states, and to read into the Constitution rights that simply are not there.

The illegitimate expansion of the power of the judiciary is a general problem that should concern all Americans who take seriously the founders' position that all power derives from the people. But especially should it concern Christians. In doing so much to help create the culture of rights, the courts have diminished the capacity of the states to legislate on matters of religion and morality, thus denying the founders' federalism and, the Christian will add, diminishing the moral strength of the nation. The Court's announcement of a right to privacy led to the invalidation of the abortion laws of fifty states. And its development of First Amendment rights led to the jurisdictional application of the establishment clause to the states and the substantive expansion of the meaning of the clause to condemn public school prayer, devotions, and other religious activities.

A judiciary in its right place would effectively free the legislative branches at all levels of government. It would, therefore, enable the American people to govern themselves consistent with the Constitution. In this circumstance, particularly the states and localities would be able to express substantive moral judgments and to allow religion a proper influence in public life.

Precisely how the judiciary should be restrained and returned to its proper role is a controversial question on which Christians will disagree. And precisely which legislation should be passed on a particular issue will also spark disagreement. But on the desirability of restraining the judiciary, and enhancing capacities of self-government, there should be general agreement.

Moreover, there should be general agreement on the worthiness of several arguments relevant to the tasks at hand. One argument is that the idea of "neutrality" should be opposed. Either that, or a vast reduction in the size of the state should be proposed. The notion that government should be absolutely neutral between religion and nonreligion might be acceptable, if the state were not so large and omnipresent. But the state has grown so vast that there is little room left for religion to flourish. So to require neutrality in public life is to squeeze religion to the side—out the door, in the case of public schools—and reduce its influence, to force it into a "separate but equal" condition. Either the public sphere must decrease and the private sphere increase, or else the state must give up the fiction of neutrality and accommodate religious belief (short, of course, of preferring a particular church or religion). Such accommodation, by the way, would clearly be consistent with the consensus on politics and religion that informed the American founding.

Christians should also be ready to press the question of whether religion is so divisive, as charged. It is not immediately clear that school prayer divides communities more than, say, football or basketball games do. Or that the posting of the Ten Commandments in public schools fractures communities more than, say, a rally held by the Ku Klux Klan. Religion—traditional religion—is too often treated as though it were bad for the health. Too many people live in a Hobbesian past. It is true that religion can divide and fracture a nation (Iran), and can lead to truly horrible scenes (Jonestown). But the issues in America are not those of Iran or Jonestown, and responsible Christians are not seeking to establish a theocracy but to ensure the moral strength of a democratic nation.

And this, ultimately, is the heart of the matter. We know that religion can survive without democracy; look at the Soviet Union, look at Poland. But can democracy survive without religion? Can it survive, that is, without becoming something else—fascism, or totalitarianism? The answer to this question will influence how we as a nation treat the place of religion in American life, whether we wish to encourage it or exclude it. Christians, of all people, should be ready with the answer.

TWO

Disentangling the Secular Humanism Debate

James Hitchcock

O NE OF THE ODD THINGS about contemporary secular humanism is the fact that so many of the people who actively sympathize with its world view also go to considerable lengths to deny its very existence. Habitually the secular media, for example, refer to it only in quotation marks, and there has been a systematic effort to dismiss the movement as merely the figment of hysterical "right wing" imaginations.

There is, however, ample evidence that the movement is real. The American Humanist Association has been in existence for many years, and its journal, *The Humanist,* is not without influence. It publishes articles by prominent people, many of whom are quite forthright in asserting that they see a basic conflict in American society between religious and secular values.

Both in 1933 and in 1973 the A.H.A. issued a *Humanist Manifesto,* each version of which explicitly denied that traditional belief in God can be a valid or healthy philosophy of life, and both of which posited a necessary conflict between "superstitious" religious belief and "enlightened" humanism. The second version also proclaimed sexual "liberation" as a necessary aspect of humanism, a proposition with which *The Humanist* magazine is also in agreement.

The 1933 manifesto was written by John Dewey, a professor at Columbia University who was possibly the most influential philosopher in American history, especially in the field of education. Signers of the 1973 document included philosophers like Sydney Hook, authors like Isaac Asimov, scientists like Francis Crick, the feminist leader Betty Friedan, the economist Gunnar Myrdal, and A. Philip Randolph, a labor leader also active in the civil rights movement.

In other words, the signers of the manifesto were far from being an eccentric fringe group in society—they were people with formidable influence. Thus to dismiss the idea of secular humanism, or the importance of the manifesto, is at best disingenuous.

The fact that such prominent people were willing to sign the document is itself significant. Public life—the arts, the professions, business, education—is full of believing Christians. Yet no such Christian manifesto has been forthcoming, and it is likely that most Christians in prominent positions, if asked to sign such a document, would refuse on the grounds that religion is a personal matter. That secular humanists behave differently is a sign of that movement's aggressive sense of mission, and it helps explain why secularists have been so successful in imposing their own view on American society.

Even despite the existence of the humanist manifestos, the movement is often dismissed as unimportant on the grounds that the signers are few in number, and membership in the A.H.A. is rather small, a good deal less than in most of the Christian churches in the United States. But, as already suggested, this dismissal is unrealistic—the signers of the manifesto and the contributors to, and readers of, humanist publications have influence far beyond their numbers.

But it would also be a mistake to equate secular humanism

merely with membership in a formal organization. At least since the 1960s, the attitudes and beliefs of the movement have been widespread in American society, in a sense even semi-official. Many people are secular humanists without knowing it, and many of those who are consciously secular in their values see no particular reason to join a formal organization. Humanist values are pervasive in much of the media, so that in a certain sense explicit humanist propaganda is superfluous.

The term "humanism" or "humanist," is one of the most slippery in the contemporary vocabulary, in part deliberately so. On one level all right-thinking people must be humanists, in that they must affirm human dignity and worth in the face of attacks on them. The majority of Christians are humanists in that they accept, and even celebrate, the great achievements of the human spirit—in art, in science, in humanitarian work. In good conscience Christians, along with other people, welcome whatever makes life more meaningful and fulfilling. The term "humanist" also has a very specific meaning, referring to those who are interested in the so-called humane studies—literature, art, music, philosophy, history.

It is the adjective "secular" which is the source of all the problems, and it is the point of secular humanism to insist that all true humanists, that is, all those who truly reverence the dignity of humanity, must be secularists. Secular humanism means exalting man at the expense of God. It is based on an assumption that, so long as the existence of God is acknowledged, man will be less than truly free. The liberation of man in some sense requires the death of God.

Secular humanism is not necessarily a formal atheism. Indeed, some secularists profess belief in God, and some are even clergy. Secular humanism can perhaps best be defined as living as though God did not exist. His existence may be formally acknowledged, but life is organized in such a way that He makes no difference. The triumph of secular humanism, to the extent that such has taken place, has been made possible by a working relationship between professed atheists and religious believers unprepared to allow their faith to influence their lives, at least their public lives, in any appreciable way.

In the practical order secular humanism can perhaps best be understood negatively—it proclaims the total emancipation of man from all divine laws, and much of its energy is expended in transgressing those laws one by one. Life is experienced as a series of "breakthroughs" against an oppressive moral order.

Some people have denied the validity of the term secular humanism on the grounds that nothing is truly secular. In this view, which is particularly held by certain sociologists of religion, man is an incurably religious creature who, although he may change the contents of his faith, will always relate to the universe in a religious way.

But most secular humanists would deny being religious in any sense of the word, and it seems presumptuous to tell them that they are, despite their vehement assertions to the contrary. It is also worth noting that this sociological understanding of religion—as a whole-hearted response to the "deeper dimensions" of the universe—itself easily becomes a kind of secular humanism. Some sophisticated humanists are glad to define religion in this way, because they can then claim that traditional forms of religion are overly narrow and confining. Since everyone is religious, there is really no need for organized religion.

The key test is specificity. The root meaning of the word "religion" is a "binding." It has to do with certain specific commitments and obligations which the individual undertakes at the behest of the deity. A religion which does not embody a specific way of life (one which may well seem narrow to those who do not profess it) is not a religion in any meaningful sense. It is a mere vague attitude of mind, which leaves the individual free to live as a secular humanist.

The roots of secular humanism date to the eighteenth-century cultural movement called the Enlightenment. As the name implies, the men of the Enlightenment thought they had discovered truths which had been previously shrouded in darkness, that darkness being precisely traditional Judaism and Christianity. It was in the eighteenth century that for the first time the idea gained currency that people ought to "outgrow" their religious beliefs, which were equated with childish superstition. At the same time organized religion was also equated with tyranny and oppression, so that the churches were accused of being enemies of human freedom and dignity. The French philosopher Voltaire's curse upon the Catholic Church—"crush the infamous thing"—defined the attitude of generations of militant secularists towards all forms of organized religion.

In the later twentieth century there has been less open warfare between religion and "science" (broadly defined) than in the eighteenth and nineteenth centuries. In part this is because secular intellectuals are inclined to be less rigidly rationalistic, more willing to admit that not everything in the universe can be encompassed by their theories; and in part because religious leaders have made often strenuous efforts to accommodate their faith to the demands of science.

However, Enlightenment attitudes of anti-religious fervor still persist. To a great extent they have shifted from the intellectual elite itself (although they are still found there) to the half-educated masses, and have worked their way into the mainstream of popular culture, especially through the mass media.

The 1960s in particular were a time of intense popular iconoclasm, and organized religion was inevitably one of the main targets of the attack. There has thus grown up a whole generation in the United States which has totally rejected even the idea of organized religion and regards the teaching and practices of traditional Christianity as false, superstitious, and oppressive of human dignity. This attitude is, as noted, held even by many people who have no idea that they espouse something which can be called an ideology.

A major part of the problem is that most such people do not realize, or do not acknowledge, that they possess any ideology at all. They have dismissed Christianity as an ideology, that is, as a body of beliefs which requires its adherents to relate to reality in a partisan and distorting way, but they regard their own anti-religious sentiments as self-evidently true. Thus such people can be tirelessly vigilant for the least signs that religion is "imposing" itself on the public order, while assuming that their own anti-religious outlook is a manifestation of freedom of expression.

The general direction of modern liberalism has been towards the expansion of the area of permissible human actions. This is especially reflected in what can now be taught in schools, as opposed to what would have been regarded as acceptable several generations ago. By a series of court decisions teachers have won wide protection for the expression of controversial political, artistic, or sexual opinions in the classroom, and the same freedom has been embodied in textbooks and other instructional materials.

Yet there has been a precisely parallel movement to restrict freedom of religious expression in public, not only in schools but in all other places supported by public money. Religion has been the one area of expression which has been restricted rather than expanded through legal action. Whereas at one time prayers, readings from the Bible, and references to the existence of God were commonplace in public classrooms, they have now been banned.

One of the lawyers most responsible for this state of affairs, Leo Pfeffer of the American Jewish Congress, has bluntly referred to it as the "triumph of secular humanism," and it is indicative of the thoroughness of that triumph that many of its agents are not themselves secular humanists but rather religious believers who have accepted, however reluctantly, the secularist view of the American Constitution. Prior to 1947 the courts did not hold that the First Amendment required the systematic expunging of every vestige of religious expression from public institutions. That position was forged through a whole series of carefully chosen court cases in which, step by step, a partisan position, inspired ultimately by hostility to organized religion, was given preferred status by the judges.

Those who have achieved this revolution have in the process fostered a double myth of neutrality—that their own motives are merely a disinterested devotion to the Constitution, and that the revolution they have created has established a benevolent neutrality fair both to believers and non-believers.

Yet some of the key figures in that revolution, for example, Supreme Court Justices William O. Douglas and Hugo Black, are known to have harbored personal animosities against organized religion, as did some of the plaintiffs in whose name suits were brought, and some of the lawyers involved, like Leo Pfeffer. In many cases the real position of the perpetrators of this judicial revolution is that organized religion is a malign social force, which must be restricted as much as possible.

It can hardly be said that the courts have mandated a state of equality between belief and non-belief when virtually all expressions of religious belief have been almost fanatically hunted down and banned from public institutions. Such a situation can only seem like "neutrality" to those who do not regard religion as important for the well being of the nation.

It is not even clear that the present situation of "neutrality" protects religion from attack through the medium of public institutions. Anti-religious plays, for example, are sometimes subsidized by public grants, and if a teacher were dismissed from a public school for using the classroom to attack religion, it is likely that "civil libertarians" would support the teacher rather than the school. (Open attacks on religion have for years been quite common in state universities, even as most such universities have not had religion departments.)

However, even when religion is not directly attacked, silence is itself a powerful form of speech. From age five to age eighteen, American children spend a majority of their waking hours, nine months of the year, in classrooms. Many then choose to continue their education into college and graduate school. To a considerable extent the entire function of education has been taken from the family and given to the schools. If, during all that considerable time, children and young people hear no mention of God, no suggestion that religion may have something important to say about the state of the universe, if they sense that teachers go to elaborate lengths to avoid religious subjects in the classroom, they inevitably draw certain conclusions—that religion is not true or relevant, possibly that it is something not altogether wholesome. This is reinforced as the student also realizes that, in most other areas of life, the modern school seeks to accommodate as many "points of view," including controversial ones, as it can.

The public schools have been a major force in the creation of a secularized society, because they have instilled in generations of students the impression that religion is a purely private matter which has no place in public life. It is an attitude which, although legally enforced only in institutions supported by public funds, comes to seem normative even for many private institutions. Thus Americans have become blind to the fact that television, for example, largely ignores religion, except for brief episodes during news programs.

Politics reflects this practical secularization in a particularly acute way. Almost all members of Congress belong to some religious group, and many of them are regular church-goers. Some are known to be quite devout. Yet even some of the devout insist on making a sharp distinction between their personal beliefs and their public stances. On the abortion issue, for example, a politician will not uncommonly say that, while he is personally opposed to the practice because of his religion, he will not "impose" his religious beliefs on other people. Hence in practice he consistently supports legalized and publicly funded abortions, even though he believes these things to be morally wrong.

Such a dichotomy between private belief and public action epitomizes secular humanism, and shows how it can be the working philosophy even of religious believers. For the formula "personally I am opposed, but . . ." rests on the assumption that religious belief cannot be a valid guide to public conduct, even when religion enlightens the individual as to the moral rightness or wrongness of a given situation.

There has so far been one ambitious attempt to read this division into the Constitution itself. In a case called *McRae* v. *Califano* (later changed to *McRae* v. *Harris*) "civil libertarians" argued that all attempts to restrict the public funding of abortion are invalid because such opposition is motivated by religious belief. The courts, at least on that occasion, rejected the argument. However, it is likely to be raised again, and it is worth noting that, if the argument were accepted, religious believers would literally be second-class citizens—barred by law from full participation in politics unless they could demonstrate that their involvement was in no way motivated by their religion. (Plaintiffs in the McRae case went so far as to hire a private detective to follow a Catholic congressman, and to read his mail, in order to determine how devout he was, and to what extent his constituents were religious believers. Plantiffs included some Protestant and Jewish groups, once again indicative of how thoroughly some religious people have accepted secular-humanist assumptions.)

Secularists often make an elaborate show of defending freedom of worship in a strict sense, supporting the rights of Jehovah's Witnesses not to have to salute the American flag, for example, or of Seventh Day Adventists not to have to work on Saturdays. But such solicitude is usually extended only to religious groups which are small and rather marginal to American society, people whose eccentricities, as it were, can be indulged. Where the "mainline" churches are concerned, the tendency has been to respond with vigilance and suspicion, as though such groups constitute a potential threat to democracy.

No respectable person at present advocates curtailing freedom of worship (although it could be severely restricted by taxing the churches and thus forcing many to close, which is already a "respectable" position). However, the aim of the secularists is precisely to define religion as a purely private and subjective matter, rather like choosing a spouse, with no legitimate public expression. This is the case not only in the political realm but, as already suggested, in education and in the mass media as well. For several decades Americans have been conditioned to think that religion is a purely "personal" thing, preferably not even to be talked about in public, a mentality which insures a secular society.

It is essential to secular humanism not to admit that it is an ideology in competition with religious ideologies for the loyalty of people and the right to guide the future direction of society, and the secularists have so far managed to have it both ways. On the one hand the Supreme Court (in *Torcaso* v. *Watkins* and *United States* v. *Seeger*) has observed that secular humanism is a religion, whose adherents have a right to the benefits of church membership (e.g., they can claim conscientious exemption from military service). But on the other hand courts have consistently denied claims that secular humanism is a religion which is given a favored place in the public schools.

It is, once again, a mistake to think of secular humanism primarily in terms of an organized and structured movement. Indeed it is precisely because it is not, while the churches are, that it can deny its own existence. Organized forms of secular humanism, like the American Humanist Association, are less influential than are countless people in sensitive positions— teachers and professors, social workers, journalists, politicians—whose outlook on life is secular and who assume secularist attitudes as normal.

The 1973 *Humanist Manifesto* was signed by several prominent "sexologists"—Albert Ellis, Lester Kirkendall, and Sol Gordon, along with Lawrence Lader, a leader in the move to legalize abortion; Allen F. Guttmacher, president of Planned Parenthood; and Joseph Fletcher, a moral theologian whose

n comfort in the hope tha
me, the family itself w
in which children can t
increasingly obvious th
helming force of a cultu
and unless social institu
n be made to support th
crumble. This too impli

elievers have a naive view o
has been foisted on ther
It is a view with two relate
requires being deferenti
y "private" matters do no

is increasingly the case tha
"private" issues. Fifty year
ought of as a policeman, it
rder and provide for th
the New Deal of the 1930s
Western world has come to
onsibility for the well-bein
e, there are no areas of lif
ude itself.
er generations had regarded
noral, it would have seemed
it agencies should pay foi
h-school students. Yet, once
been identified as medically
at government will promote

ions which perhaps ought to
g political. If nothing else,
r how public money is spent,
y moral.
religious believers are often

main achievement has been to rationalize all aspects of the contemporary "sexual revolution."

This link between secular humanism and sexual "liberation" is scarcely accidental. For it is in the area of sexuality that secularist values are now pushed with the greatest fervor, and where the conflict between secularism and traditional religion is most acute.

Because it is highly personal, sexuality has always been perhaps the single most sensitive area of human life, and hence it has always been the most sensitive area of morality as well. People experience the force of sexual prohibitions in a very direct way, and they tend to experience a considerable degree of guilt when they transgress the laws of sexual morality.

Thus sexuality has become perhaps the most crucial test case in the spread of secular humanism, because it is here that human beings who seek to be truly "free" of binding laws assert most forthrightly their independence. If they succeed there, most other declarations of moral independence will be relatively easy. Sexuality has become the crucial test case of the proposition that there are no divine laws binding human beings, that a subjective sense of "self-fulfillment" should be the only criterion of right and wrong.

The 1933 *Humanist Manifesto* was prudently silent about matters of sexuality; it was still a rather conservative time, morally. By 1973, however, secular humanists had seen fit to proclaim the sexual revolution as an integral part of their creed and to declare boldly that human beings are bound by no higher code.

Indeed, once this freedom is proclaimed, it follows that people are not only free to indulge in a wide range of hitherto forbidden sexual behavior, they are practically obligated to do so, because not to do so reveals that they are still prisoners of an outworn morality. Secular humanism aims at the complete and unlimited development of all "human potential." Hence it must continually batter down all remaining restraints on human conduct, in order both to destroy all psychological

taboos and to demonstrate the full extent o
dom."

Abortion involves questions both of sexual
the dignity of human life. Increasingly, the
morality is becoming as sensitive as sexualit
abortion but also infanticide and euthanasia a
respectable people. Ironically, self-proclaimed
ends by becoming anti-human, as some influent
rary spokesmen now insist that human beings as
no special claim over other species, that a hum
example, might have less claim to life than a fu
bear. (Such a position was argued in 1983 in an
official journal of the American Academy of Pec

Many Christians, although remaining faithful
sexual morality, also tend to see it as purely "priva
not a real social issue. Abortion, however, is
private—the traditional teaching is that it involve
taking of a human life, a matter about which the
citizens cannot be indifferent. For this reason a
become one of the most bitterly contested moral i
day, and will continue to be so.

It is no accident that the Nobel Prize-winnin
Francis Crick was a signer of the 1973 *Humanis*
because one influential form of secular humanism
scientism which rules out religion on the grounds t
scientific. It is a point of view which pervades, fo
Carl Sagan's popular television series, *Cosmos*. Fo
type of scientific mind, man through science has bec
and he can do whatever he wishes. (Crick has ga
notoriety through his proposal that no child be
declared a human being until two weeks after birth
that time any child could be killed to suit the wis
parents or the attending physicians.)

It is likewise no mere coincidence that the "grandn
feminism," Betty Friedan, should also have been o
signers, because radical feminism is inherently secu

Parents have for a long time take
whatever happens outside the ho
remain a nurturing environment
trained in the proper way. But it i
the family is no match for the overv
which is itself thoroughly seculal
tions, both public and private, ca
family, the latter will progressively
an inescapable political agenda.

Unfortunately, many religious b
the political process, one which
precisely by the secular humanists.
claims—that a pluralistic society
about one's views, and that purel
belong in the public arena.

To consider the second first, it
there are no longer any genuinely
ago the government was mainly th
purpose to preserve domestic
national defense. Since the time of
however, government all over the
be thought of as having total resp
of its citizens. This being the ca
where it may not legitimately intr

Thus even if Americans of earli
the practice of contraception as
bizarre to them that governme
distributing contraceptives to hig
the practice of contraception has
desirable, it follows inevitably th
and encourage it.

Hence all kinds of moral quest
be private end up by becomin
politics is a constant struggle ov
and all such choices are ultimate

In this connection orthodox

accused of being absolutists who try to impose their morality on everyone else, of not properly respecting American pluralism. The implication is that pluralism is a system in which diverse groups voluntarily refrain from pushing their own views too hard, lest they tread on the toes of their neighbors.

In reality, pluralism is precisely the opposite. It is of the essence of a pluralistic society that, since there is no commonly accepted standard for what is true or false, every group must push as hard as it can for its own positions. Limits are imposed on this only by other groups pushing equally hard in the other direction.

No effective social movement of the past quarter century— the civil rights movement, the peace movement, feminism, environmentalism—has been successful by being voluntarily deferential to other groups. Each has achieved its goals through being militant and often uncompromising. This is a rule which many religious believers have not as yet learned.

Much of the time politics consists in battles which seem only tangentially related to religion, or about which religious believers legitimately disagree—domestic spending programs and foreign policy, mainly. However, to an increasing degree politics is also coming to be concerned with issues of a kind which go to the heart of religious and moral values. Among the more obvious questions are the following:

—Should the practice of abortion, infanticide, and euthanasia be permitted under the law, and if so, should they be supported by government funding?

—Must religion be excluded from public institutions under the First Amendment? Does the First Amendment also forbid, to the same extent, using public institutions to promote irreligion?

—What is the proper balance between the authority of the family in the lives of children and that of public agencies, especially schools?

—Should public schools attempt to inculcate moral values in children, and if so of what kind?

—What rights do parents have when they object to the values enshrined in existing educational institutions? How far can government go in regulating religious schools?

—What is a family, and should families have a special place in law and public policy? Should the law continue to give to marriage a status which it denies to extra-legal relationships? Should it be the aim of public policy to encourage stable families? Should public policy assume that two-parent families are healthier for children than one-parent families? Should homosexual relationships be given a status equal to that of marriage?

—Should the government mandate and enforce "affirmative action" programs on behalf of homosexuals?

This is only a partial list, but it illustrates the fact that, whether or not they wish to do so, religious believers cannot help getting involved in politics. To pretend that religion is a purely private matter which has nothing to do with public life is already to concede victory to the enemies of religion and traditional moral values. Religious believers, in short, have a political agenda.

At present the single greatest obstacle to the realization of such an agenda is the passivity, and often the confusion, of believers themselves. Now, as perhaps never before in American history, it is overwhelmingly the case that the only thing required for evil to triumph is for good people to do nothing.

THREE

"Secular Humanism" or "The American Way?"

Joseph Sobran

W E HEAR ENDLESSLY of the importance of "compassion" and "understanding," and it is not at all to dispute the importance of these things to observe that they are far more difficult to achieve than their frequent and facile invocation would lead us to think. Compassion is easy to work up for a moment, when one reads, for instance, a news story about a little boy battered to death by his mother and her lover; it is harder to sustain for a constantly complaining relative.

As for understanding, people can live together and yet talk at cross-purposes for years on end. Deciphering language whose meaning seems clear, especially when it comes from people who seem innocent of all subtlety, can be hard. It can be especially hard when you already despise them and judge them to be far below yourself in intellectual caliber. All the more reason to make the effort, beginning with the self-reminder that an effort may in fact be necessary.

These ruminations began one day when, my children being out of the house for a few days, I pondered Jean-Paul Sartre's remark that "hell is other people." Sartre was, in my judgment, a profound fool, and I began to wonder, nonetheless, what he would have meant by that. He chose to regard other people as hellish; he chose not to have children, his paramour, Simone de Beauvoir, having made a point of saying publicly that she had had an abortion. What a pair. They had ruled out the great experiences celebrated by Shakespeare, the real risks of living in others; they had chosen, on doctrinaire principle, to be like Lear in Act I, aborting their progeny instead of investing themselves in a new life, imposing raw will on others and insisting that this infernal choice epitomized the human condition. The Lear of Act V was presumably guilty, in their eyes, of bad faith.

But were they so odd? I had just taken my children to the latest James Bond movie, the only film in town that didn't seem to feature Bo Derek in a bubble bath, and it struck me that Bond's world was much like theirs, for all its *haut bourgeois* sheen: a world of mayhem, where lust was "liberated" from lasting union and the encumbrance of children. We had had to sit through not only the helicopter and submarine and ski-slope adventures, which was after all what we'd come for, but the inevitable, PG-level lechery; parental guidance now casually includes allowing children to be shown that "sex," as we call it, need not be cursed with issue.

At what point did it suddenly go without saying that this is life? When did the dirty joke cease being a joke, and become a lifestyle? It is one thing to take a controversial position, but another to pretend it's not even controversial. This is the new hypocrisy: the suppression of any admission that there can be two points of view, even as we pretend we are somewhat daring in taking one of them. Suddenly we find a new constitution in effect, when we can't even recall having taken a vote, much less held a debate.

The press has been full of scornful articles on fundamentalists who attack what they call "secular humanism." The articles put the phrase between quotation marks, deriding the very idea that there is such a *thing* as secular humanism; they contrive to make the idea sound like a lunatic fantasy, akin to delusions that fluoridated water is a Communist conspiracy.

Well, we need not call the phenomenon "secular humanism" (though men like Leo Pfeffer, not the Jerry Falwells, coined the phrase, applying it to themselves). But it is disingenuous to deny that there is such a phenomenon at all.

One very subtle and effective technique of evading debate is to pretend that there can really be nothing to argue about. Part of this technique is the refusal to accept any opponent's label for one's own position. The moment one admits having a special position, that position becomes vulnerable. Much more adroit to represent the attribution of any definable position to an opponent's *gaucherie.*

And it is true that a label like "secular humanism" can become a catch-all for whatever we disapprove of. Still, it is unlikely that even the coarsest Bible-thumper is expressing a disapproval only of something whose existence is confined to his imagination. If his perception is crude or distorted, we ought to acknowledge, in all fairness, that he nonetheless perceives *something*; and we ought to take the trouble to define it accurately.

The people the fundamentalists call secular humanists like to say that they "avoid labels," and ordinarily they are no doubt eager to do so; as if to suggest that they are nothing but a random collection of individualists whose essence is so very refined that the words have not yet been coined that can capture it. But this may be too self-flattering, and too self-serving. When it suits their purposes they *can* find labels for themselves. One of the targets of Moral Majority wrath, TV producer Norman Lear, has formed an organization called People for the American Way.

As a rule, liberals (to use a label not quite out of use) scorn the arrogance of anyone who posits a single "American Way." If conservatives do so, liberals are quick to speak of McCarthyism and intolerance. Likewise the liberal priest Robert Drinan, in his inaugural speech as president of the Americans for Democratic Action, called the Moral Majority and its ilk "enemies of this country"—a piece of invective not permitted to those enemies. As so often happens, those who demand tolerance for themselves turn out less willing, once they find a safe perch, to extend tolerance to others.

This is only natural, and natural in a sense that need not suggest the baseness of fallen nature. The Anglican Richard Baxter once laid down the rule, "Tolerate the tolerable," implying, as Samuel Johnson observed, that there must also be a category of things not tolerable. The question becomes, What view of life is the liberal side upholding under which the Moral Majority must be deemed intolerable?

The question is complicated by the fact that Drinan, like Falwell, is a clergyman, and therefore presumably not a "secular humanist." Or is it that simple? While he was in Congress, Drinan fought extraordinarily hard, even vitupera-tively, for legal abortion and even for federal funding for abortions, subordinating the doctrines of his religion to the imperatives of "a woman's choice." Can it be that a Catholic priest would willingly pave the way for the killing of unborn human beings, each of whom has not only a moral right to live, but an immortal soul?

Perhaps. Drinan can always take the familiar line (I expect he did take it) that he is "personally opposed" to abortion even as he fought for the *civil* right of a woman to "control her own body." We may even lay aside, though not fail to note, the amazing disparity of passion between his political commit-ment to abortion and his moral opposition to the actual performance of the act.

Even so, the question nags: How can a merely *legal* right to do an admittedly evil thing (for this is what "personally opposed" must mean) impose such a *moral* imperative to tolerate, and subsidize, the evil thing itself? One might passionately favor states' rights, under the federal system, to the extent of opposing a federal anti-lynch law; but surely, in that case, one would feel obliged, as vehemently as possible, to make clear one's moral abhorrence of lynching. The people in Congress and elsewhere who "personally oppose" abortion do nothing of the kind. It is fair to infer—actually it is silly to doubt—that their expressed opposition to abortion is formalistic only.

Put otherwise, it is nearly impossible to imagine any of them trying to discourage a woman, on moral grounds, from making the choice they have struggled to legalize. None of them has audibly laid down moral criteria for abortion. None of them has confronted the simple physical agony suffered by the child in late abortions. None of them expressed revulsion at the acts, perhaps homicidal even under the loose guidelines of the Supreme Court, committed by Doctors Kenneth Edelin and William Waddill.

We can hardly believe, in the face of such evidence, that the term "pro-abortion" is less apt than the term "pro-choice." They may pretend merely to be engaged in sharply distinguishing the moral and legal realms; but if that were true, they would make the distinction in practice, not just in verbal *formulae* which have no practical consequences.

Put in broader terms, it is clear that for at least many of them, there is no effective distinction between these realms. They identify the moral and legal realms as thoroughly, at least in their practical conduct and emotional experience, as any Prohibitionist who ever thought that what is intrinsically immoral must be made illegal, and that whatever is legally tolerated must be considered as having a moral sanction.

In sociological terms, the modernizing process is thought to consist largely in "differentiating" categories of human action. One of the basic modern differentiations has been the separation of church and state; and pro-abortionists claim the sanction of the modernizing principle by asserting that legalizing abortion is only a way of extending the church-state distinction. In the words of the American Civil Liberties Union, which has fought against the Hyde Amendment on constitutional grounds, limitations on abortion serve "no secular purpose"—a phrase and a principle earlier laid down by the Supreme Court.

But the modernizing principle, perhaps perfectly valid in itself, is fraudulently invoked if it is used to mean an illicit secularization of all of life, including what ought to belong to the sacred. In a sense the modernizing principle can be said to derive from the words of Christ: "Render unto Caesar the things that are Caesar's, and unto God the things that are God's." St. Augustine himself elaborated the distinction, differentiating the earthly and heavenly cities.

But no Christian has ever admitted, and until recently few American liberals have ever held, that this distinction requires us, *qua* citizens of the earthly city, to act as if the heavenly city were less real than the one we presently inhabit. This has changed. In Europe it began to change with the French Revolution, in which social anticlericalism was wildly mixed with hatred of religion—with, ultimately, the hatred of God explicitly avowed by Sartre in recent times. The Russian Revolution, among others, set out to abolish religion altogether, with no pretense of merely separating the secular and sacred realms: for Communism, to this day, the state comprehends all of human existence.

But in the American tradition such claims by the secular have never been officially adopted. Nor are they today: but they have been furtively advanced, under color of separationism. And now we find them being ever more boldly, if confusedly, advanced, still under the aegis of keeping church and state separate.

Pursuant to its suit against the Hyde Amendment, the ACLU inspected Congressman Henry Hyde's mail and offered its heavy component of religious expressions as evidence that the Hyde Amendment, limiting federal funding of abortions, was illicitly motivated by non-secular purposes. An ACLU agent even testified that he had followed Hyde to mass and observed him receiving Communion—a further taint on the Amendment. This could only be considered evidence that the Amendment was unconstitutional if specifically religious motives are somehow forbidden by the Constitution to influence public policy. This is a historically novel doctrine: Sunday "blue laws" are only one sign that the American people have never understood their polity and its theoretical basis as the ACLU understands them. (The ACLU has also sued to force Catholic hospitals to make their facilities available for the performance of abortions.)

Another sign of the new understanding appeared in the election of 1980, when liberal columnists like Anthony Lewis of the *New York Times* accused clergymen like Falwell and Cardinal Medeiros of Boston of *violating the Constitution* in taking political positions. Several conservatives quickly replied that this charge had never been thrown at the many clergymen who had taken liberal positions on war, civil rights, and nuclear energy. But the more fundamental point was that the liberals were implicitly interpreting the constitutional command that "Congress shall make no law respecting an establishment of religion" as, in effect, an actual abridgment of the clergy's own "free exercise" of religion. Lewis, to his credit, admitted that this was true, and retracted the charge. The remarkable thing was that he had made it at all: a fact that bespoke the impulse toward total secularization we are concerned with here.

Again, when it appeared that a Mormon federal appeals judge, Marion Callister, might be called on to rule on the constitutionality of the deadline extension for ratification of the Equal Rights Amendment, liberals like the columnist Ellen Goodman demanded that Callister be disqualified—because the Mormon Church officially opposes ERA. This was too much for Leo Pfeffer, the nation's foremost avowed secular humanist: in a splendidly impartial display of principle, he wrote a letter to the *New York Times* in defense of Callister, pointing out that his disqualification would amount to an unconstitutional "religious test" for public office.

These are only a few examples of the steadily-growing claims of all-out secularizers for the exclusion of all religious influence from American public life. We may also mention the growing boldness of purely secular agencies, like the *Times,* in demanding the reform of churches along secular lines: they think nothing of campaigning for the ordination of women or denouncing ecclesiastical disciplines by churches against their own members or calling on the churches to alter doctrinal positions on moral issues like birth control. As long as they can find (and publicize) one dissident member of a faith, they see nothing amiss in their leaping into the fray on his (or her) side. The affair of Sonia Johnson, the excommunicated Mormon feminist, is a case in point: Mrs. Johnson enjoyed highly sympathetic media coverage, it meaning nothing to the media, apparently, that this was the internal affair of an institution with doctrines and organization of its own. Again and again we encounter the implicit demand that the churches reform themselves on lines stipulated by secularist forces.

At this point the Moral Majoritarian may innocently feel that the case is pretty well closed: the secular humanists consistently show their tremendous arrogance. But putting it this way may be, for our purposes, premature. What is it that these secular humanists, to call them that, feel, deep in their hearts, that they are doing?

Making all allowances for hypocrisy, we must still remember that the most destructive people may be quite sincere. In any case, the people we are discussing don't call themselves secular humanists, and don't even think of themselves as such. They are not conscious of dishonestly promoting a special creed; they are not conscious of holding such a creed at all. I know of no evidence whatever that they talk among themselves in a dialect very different from the one they use in public. That must tell us something. How do they see themselves?

I venture to say that they think of themselves not as scheming atheists, but, precisely, as upholders of the American Way. When they cite the First Amendment, they mean it—at least as they grasp the import of the First Amendment. The simplest explanation is that they think of it as containing the radiant essence of the Constitution, and of our basic political premises.

They think of religion as an irrational force, capable, when it interferes in secular life (and they assume that its influence is properly described, on the whole, as interference), of producing great harm. At the very least, they feel that it consists in claiming a special "pipeline to God" and a "monopoly on Truth" that renders rational social discourse next to impossible. We can only converse fruitfully with each other, they feel, if we confine our public discourse to premises we can all accept—which means that anything purporting to be divine revelation has no place in that discourse. They do feel that the Judeo-Christian tradition contains many excellent things, which can, of course, be held without subscribing to that tradition as a whole, or on its own terms.

This is the key, I think. They feel that there is a moral consensus about matters like murder, theft, charity, and the like, and that we can all peaceably agree on these regardless of how we regard the tradition as a whole. They therefore welcome the political utterances of the clergy—so long as, and only so long as, these are confined to areas of consensus between Christians and non-Christians.

But of course there is a catch here, and they don't notice it. Their notion of "consensus" is reductive, in a way particularly convenient to them. It means that the area of agreement is defined almost exclusively by themselves. If they reject a certain part of the Judeo-Christian tradition, then religious people are forbidden to bring that part into public discourse. In fact religious people must behave, within the secular arena, as if that part didn't exist. To behave otherwise is to impose the views of a minority on everyone. The views of the majority, by definition, are those views acceptable to liberals, "secular humanists," or whatever we are to call them: they are a recognizable body, almost a sect, even if we hardly know what to call them.

Religious people, in other words, are required to play the political game by rules laid down by their adversaries. And this, the most fundamental rule of all, is supposed to have been the first and original principle of the Republic. That is the meaning of the constant appeal to the First Amendment. But—a critically important fact—this Amendment is not itself subject to amending. It is supposed to have exactly the kind of dogmatic status which Christians claim for divine revelation. Its origin is never fully explained; it (in its liberal interpretation) is simply posited as the condition of all possible political existence—and, as the claims of politics expand to include all human life, of all human existence on earth. (If there is any other dimension of human existence, it is not to be considered.)

In this way, the liberal/secular humanist ground rules seem to those who accept them unquestioningly to supply the basis for all manner of further claims on other institutions. Discussion of the sacred and *its* claims are, ironically, foreclosed *by the First Amendment itself.* That is why liberals, as Basile Uddo has remarked in a splendid essay on the American Civil Liberties Union, can unblushingly ban religious expression from public institutions, establishing new forms of virtual censorship—in addition to the proscriptions against religion in politics I mentioned earlier.

The repercussions are enormous. They affect all institutions, public as well as private. I have already mentioned the casual demand that religious bodies abide by secular standards: if this can be required, it should be an easy matter to require as much of institutions that straddle the secular and the sacred. If human life itself must not be regarded as sacred, if the family must not be understood as of divine institution, then there is nothing to stop the political order from washing over its banks to reform these too, redefining them at its convenience. Property and wealth, of course, are politically up for grabs. Public education need observe no restraints except against prayer and Christmas carols; there is no reason to regard sex education as beyond its province, since neither religious nor parental authority in these matters need be regarded as inviolable.

Politics, in short, loses all its old limitations, and subject only to the taboo on religion, becomes the arena within which all human destiny is worked out. The state becomes a *de facto* god. No other human relations—certainly not those of the family—can claim priority over those of state and citizen. What with newly posited children's and women's rights, the state may even assume the power of interfering in family relations, ostensibly to protect one citizen against the arbitrary action of another.

Inevitably this means that there is no authority above man himself. Practically, it means the divinization of political man, man acting through the state. All authority, all social order, all human relations claiming divine sanction must be treated as fictions, and probably mischievous fictions at that—else we violate the separation of church and state.

Man, Sartre tells us, is himself "the desire to be God." Under the liberal regime this is never openly admitted, and can't be. But it comes to the same thing. We are getting the ideology of the French Revolution under the guise and forms of the American tradition.

I repeat, there is no reason to suppose this is all a diabolically conscious process, cunningly disguised by its avatars. There is every reason to accept their protestations that they believe they merely represent "the American Way." Norman Lear can use his TV sit-coms to propagandize for sexual liberation, abortion, and democratic socialism without feeling that he is doing anything any reasonable person would deem controversial. But his "reasonable person" is Jerry Falwell's "secular humanist." They are talking about the same thing, and merely disagreeing over labels—though "merely" is hardly the word for a disagreement that issues from radically different philosophic frameworks.

Lear might well contend that his framework enjoys more intellectual respectability than Falwell's—and so, in a sense, it would. The very word "intellectual" has taken on a special coloration: it refers almost exclusively to the "secular humanists" themselves, those who make it a principle never to advert to divine authority in their public life. For them, man achieved his independence with the Enlightenment, and Harold Rosenberg's ironic phrase "the herd of independent minds" has an enormous resonance. To be an intellectual, in the current sense, is not necessarily to have any *personal* intellectual distinction at all: it is merely to belong to the party, or "herd," that rejects traditional religion and seeks humanistic authority.

And how are such intellectuals to deal with non-intellectuals—i.e., the religious? By force. It may be disguised; it usually is, for purposes of liberal decorum. But since there is no reasoning with people who reject the "First Amendment" premises of rational discourse, the political prescriptions of the enlightened—abortion, say, or racial busing—may have to be imposed by fiat, with whatever compulsion is feasible and necessary. The judiciary, custodian of the secular humanist ground rules, has served as a theocratic priesthood which, in the name of the American Constitution, has successfully circumvented popular politics to realize much of the liberal agenda. By such devices has the party of the New American Way managed to read its opponents out of the American polity.

But this is changing. Conservative forces are becoming far more sophisticated about the real motives and *modus operandi* of their adversaries. The very outcry over "secular humanism," on both sides, shows that the conservatives have caught the scent.

Religious, philosophic, and metaphysical questions are all important, but the real battleground is the family—the level at which most people are directly touched. The family's weakened status could never have been simply imposed from above. To a great extent, alas, it springs from popular demand. Fornication, adultery, and abortion are nothing new, nor was their popularity ever confined to judges.

But these old sins are now being institutionalized as "rights," and more and more people sense that what once appeared as attractive options are now forming part of a new and malign political order in which the reality of the family must crumble before the reality of sheer state power. What was once the sanctuary of private affection now falls under the domain of raw force. The French secularist tradition that begot Sartre has been more lucid about this than the gentler Anglo-Saxon tradition under which the abolition of man (to use C.S. Lewis's phrase) took on the aspect of liberal modernization.

Sartre said boldly that every man is alone, and that society is agglutinated by terror. Our society is a long way from the totalitarian systems Sartre delighted in, but it has its own uneasiness. We are beginning to realize that the humanitarian claims of "compassion," under which the state claims more and more of our substance, mask an order based on compulsion, and therefore fear—if only the fear of agencies like the Internal Revenue Service and those acronymic organs of state "social welfare."

At the moment it is awkward to dispute the universalist claims of "compassion" in the name of the more concrete and humble loves of the family. The conservative forever finds himself in the position of King Lear's daughter Cordelia— condemned for hardheartedness for refusing to enter a competition of extravagant professions. In an age that denies man's nature (because it suppresses the mention of God), we are expected to join the new political creation that will improve the handiwork of the Creator by subjecting it to larger and larger organization, driven by what Robert Frost called "that tenderer-than-thou collectivistic regimenting love with which the modern world is being swept."

In the last analysis we must have a footing on which to stand as we say No to the all-swallowing state. Such a footing requires us simply to speak in the language of the Divine, in spite of all the taboos imposed by a false secularization. The word "godless" has been deliberately made to sound quaint and out of place in political discourse, for the very reason that it is most apposite. Terms like "secular humanism" are similarly forbidden (if only by ridicule) for the very good reason that they effectively identify, if only approximately, the specific outlook we are up against.

We must insist that we are all mere men, not gods; we are not even God collectively, or in our political representatives. We are *under* God. We are His creatures, his frail, sinful creatures, made to love each other in simple though difficult ways; as husbands and wives, parents and children, neighbors among neighbors, friends among friends, and, yes, citizens among citizens, in all relations recognizing that we stand under judgment. If we try to be more than mere men, we will only become less, the order of love and justice giving way to the order of sheer arbitrary power. Whoever tries to change the social fabric in which we are knitted together by God will only lead us into chaos. Within the social order God made us for, we can have contentment and occasional joy. Outside it, only lust, greed, fear, and despair.

Those to whom this view of things sounds impossibly backward are what are meant by the phrase "secular humanists." It is worth noticing that they have their own kind of fear: they describe their adversaries not only demeaningly, as "reactionaries," but as actually "dangerous." As they should: for those who still belong to the order of love actually pose a fatal menace to the New American Way. The secular humanists deplore any talk of a "Communist menace," because they look on Communism as an essentially rational (though no doubt occasionally brutal) social principle, akin somehow to their own, and therefore eligible for "dialogue" and "negotiation." After all, Communism never adverts to the supernatural. It is only a variant of secular humanism, which is why secular humanists remain far more scandalized by religious wars and persecutions than by the continuing oppressions (including the persecution of religion) of the Communist regimes.

This is why the secular humanists have resisted distinguishing between authoritarian and totalitarian regimes: even to recognize the difference—including the unique totalitarian feature of armed borders, at which people are shot for trying to escape—is automatically to admit the special monstrosity, to ordinary people, of states that assume the status of divinities. The furtive sympathy of many "liberals" for Communism is alternately hotly denied and openly expressed, according to the change of seasons. Stalin, Mao, and Castro have all had their vogues, with American professors and senators returning from brief visits to exult that "they have much to teach us." What they ultimately have to teach us is what depths godless man can sink to. That those are exalted as heights tells us all we really need to know about the godless men of our own society.

This, at any rate, is how I decipher the current debates over "secular humanism," "creationism," "the separation of church and state," and so forth. The precise words have no final importance. But in the field of God and man, society and the world, they serve to alert us to certain decisive alignments, whose membership on both sides I hope I have described and analyzed accurately enough, without concealing my own partiality to the side I think is finally in the right, even if it sometimes seems to be losing the immediate arguments or simply swinging at the air. In fact the very deficit of obvious intellectual firepower on the "Moral Majority" side seems to me to testify to its valor; when men like the Reverend Falwell risk ridicule and disgrace, along with bitter vilification, I am reminded principally of the wisdom of the God he and I adore, Who has revealed that the last shall be first, and that He has chosen the foolish things of this world to confound the wise.

FOUR

On Parents, Children, and the Nation-State

Allan C. Carlson

T HE CLASH OF WORLD VIEWS now seen within the United States is not a unique historical development. Bitter divisions over the role that religion should play in the public sphere and over the meaning and importance of the family relative to the state have emerged in other Western countries during this century. These earlier experiences offer both lessons and warnings that are useful in understanding America's current predicament.

The Lessons of France and Germany

In the years between World Wars I and II, for example, France was a deeply divided nation. The ensuing domestic struggle over the shape of national "culture" tore the French social fabric to shreds.

On the one side stood the secularists, who strove to drive religion out of public and intellectual life. Claiming devotion to the "Jacobin" virtues of the French Revolution, they advanced the principles of privacy and modernity against the old family structure and the "archaic" moral values sustained by the churches. Their most militant arm, the Freemasons, enjoyed a significant jump in membership during the 1920s, while a still larger cadre—the underpaid, pacifistic, and anti-clerical state primary school teachers—warred daily against religious influence in every city and village. But while constantly mobilized for action and deeply committed to the politics of the radical left, this latter group actually saw its real influence fall as the number of government-funded secondary schools declined.

On the other side were the Roman Catholics, standing for the cultural primacy of revealed religion. As national consensus decayed, Christian parents began moving their children out of the secularizing state schools and into church-sponsored "free" schools. Reflecting their migration, the number of such academies on the secondary level soared, from 632 in 1918 to 1,420 twenty years later. This alternative system claimed its own religiously-grounded curricula, its own textbooks, and its own version of the history and politics of France.

The result, predictably, was a nation wrenched apart and the emergence of almost two distinct races of Frenchmen, with very different historical villains and heroes, mutually unrecognizable political and moral vocabularies, and wholly antagonist assumptions about the basic purposes of individual and national life. "Churchmen and free thinkers were so carried away by the bitterness of their disagreements," historian Theodore Zeldin reports, "that they became incapable of understanding each other...."[1] By the late 1930s, both sides of this cultural divide held deep reservations about the sacrifices they would be prepared to make for their nation. "It was not a case of my country right or wrong, or my country Left or Right," historian Paul Johnson writes, "but a case of whose country—mine or theirs."[2] This internally divided France collapsed under the German military assault of May, 1940.

Ironically, Germany itself suffered during the interwar period from a similar, but far more pervasive conflict of world views. Reflecting deep regional, religious, and class divisions, Weimar Germany emerged after World War I as a "pluralistic" society where the public sphere was necessarily left amoral, or valueless. According to historian Rainer Baum, Germans shared no common vision of "the good society" rooted in the fabric of family life, faith, and community which could govern society-wide questions of right or wrong. Instead, they inherited a political culture drenched with "idealisms" and constant appeals to "higher purposes," but incapable of defining itself as a morally compelling collective endeavor. Given the resulting "privatization" of virtue, German society became marked by widespread moral subjectivity, while the German people stood before each other as ethical strangers. Appeals to "values" were transformed into mere propaganda. Pure legality replaced religiously-grounded morality as the guide to public action.

The Nazi takeover brought this process to its culmination. The SS officer emerged as the model of the cool, self-confident, post-religious man who consciously strove to resist devotion to any transcendence, who set out to dominate the world without the crutch of any moral belief. In this milieu, the family was easily discarded as the nurturing cell of society, to be replaced by the state. Heinrich Himmler's *Lebensborn* decree of October, 1939, set up breeding farms for "ideal Aryans," while female SS officers scoured the concentration camps for "Aryan-type" children to stock them. According to Baum, Germany's involvement in World War II "affirmed nothing" because the nation "shared nothing." The resulting "mountains of corpses were [considered] just so much dirt," Baum writes, because in the value vacuum that Germany had become "they had been defined as sheer matter when still alive. . . ."[3]

America's "Higher Sanction"

By way of contrast, the United States was until recently among the more fortunate of countries. While a land of immigrants counting scores of distinct ethnic groups, this nation evidenced a unique core of common values focused on religious faith and family, which gave it clear moral identity. "It was religion that gave birth to the English colonies in America," the French visitor Alexis de Tocqueville observed in the 1830s. "One must never forget that." He added that while voluntarily kept distinct from the political sphere, "Christianity has kept a strong hold over the minds of Americans, and . . . its power is not just that of a philosophy which has been examined and accepted, but that of a religion believed in without discussion." Although embracing "an infinite variety of ceaselessly changing . . . sects," Christianity remained "an established and irresistible fact which no one seeks to attack or defend." He noted that while travellers who visited North America differed on many points, "they all agree that [moral values] are infinitely stricter [here] than anywhere else."

The American family system was also the object of de Tocqueville's awe. In place of the aristocratic presumptions and formal patriarchy still present in Europe, he argued, there stood the new American family, resting on equality, where "every word a son addresses to his father has a tang of freedom, familiarity, and tenderness all at once. . . ." Siblings were no longer stratified by birth, the French observer noted, but rather were equal before the law, so that "the affectionate and frank intimacy of childhood easily takes root. . . ."

The relationship between the sexes in America impressed him. In Europe, de Tocqueville wrote, there were those who, "confusing the divergent attitudes of the sexes, claim to make of man and woman creatures who are, not only equal, but actually similar." The result, though, was "feeble men and unseemly women." Far superior, he suggested, was the American approach, where the "great principle of political economy"—the division of labor—had been usefully applied. Americans "think that nature, which created such great differences between the physical and moral constitution of men and women, clearly intended to give their diverse faculties a diverse employment; and they consider that progress consists not in making dissimilar creatures do roughly the same things but in giving both a chance to do their job as well as possible." Among Americans, he noted, marriage was considered a freely entered contract, but one that both parties were strictly bound to fulfill. This fact accounted for "the strong distaste" of Americans toward divorce and adultery. The Frenchman concluded that while American democracy loosened old communal and hierarchical ties, it tightened natural ones and brought the immediate family members closer together.[4]

The echoes of this implicit celebration of an America resting on common moral values could be heard for another 120 years. A statement remarkably similar to de Tocqueville's came as late as 1957, this time from Walt Whitman Rostow, professor of economic history at the Massachusetts Institute of Technology. Beginning in 1955, he had directed for M.I.T.'s Center for International Studies a "fundamental re-examination" of American society and institutions, a project funded by the Carnegie Corporation. In an address summarizing the results of his work, Rostow insisted that there was still a classic "American style." It was rooted, he argued, in the unique historical mixture of seventeenth-century Protestantism, the eighteenth-century Enlightenment, and "the cumulative experiences and myths" which Americans had built upon them. The fused Calvinist and Deist traditions, he stated, had cast America up as the City on the Hill, a nation set apart from other lands, with a "higher sanction and an altogether special dimension of ideological experiment and . . . leadership." From the beginning, Rostow insisted, the United States had identified nationhood "with a commitment to strive for good purposes." There even remained, he stated, "a sense in which we have continued to identify church and state."

Domestically, Rostow affirmed that families, churches and voluntary associations worked "to ramify and to weave a highly individualistic and mobile population into a firm social fabric," exhibiting "a widening area of common values." Long-term social trends such as suburbanization and bureaucratization, he argued, further increased "the social homogeneity of the American population." Even more recent shifts in American values helped to reinforce the American commitment to the family. Higher real incomes allowed "the option of increased leisure, earlier marriages, and more children. . . ." The insecurities of the Cold War era had increased Americans' "concern with values which transcend the vicissitudes of a life span—notably family and religion." Even the "welfare state" mentality was reflected "in phenomena as palpable as the birth rate" increase during the 1950s.[5]

Rostow concluded that the core values exhibited by the American nation in the post-World War II era had not changed since the country's founding. In his view, religious faith, strong family bonds, and moral probity remained the distinguishing marks of "The American."

The Demise of the American System

But then, something went terribly wrong. Statistical evidence began mounting during the 1960s and 70s which suggested that American family life was malfunctioning. The nation's divorce rate, for example, tripled between 1958 and 1978, while the marriage rate in 1980 stood at its lowest level in forty years. The number of divorced persons per 1000 married persons climbed from 35 in 1960 to 100 by 1980; among black women, the increase was from 78 to 257. The U.S. fertility rate (births per 1000 women aged 15-44) fell from 122.7 in 1957 to 66.7 in 1975, reflecting a rapid American retreat from childbearing. Over the same few years, the nation's illegitimacy ratio (illegitimate births per 100 live births) tripled. Of the 3.5 million children born in the U.S. in 1979, 17 percent were to unmarried women; among black Americans, the figure was 55 percent, almost three times the figure from the late 1950s. Four out of every ten out-of-wedlock births in 1979 were to teenage girls, who commonly became children raising children. The incidence of human abortion increased from an estimated 100,000 illegal abortions annually during the late 1950s to 615,000 in 1973 (the first year when the procedure was legal in every state) to over 1.5 million in 1982. In that year, an estimated one million American children lived on the streets, as many as a third of them supporting themselves as prostitutes.

Behind these massive changes in human behavior and familial ties lay equally rapid shifts in national mores. As late as 1967, 85 percent of the parents of college-aged-children condemned premarital sex as morally wrong. By 1981, 61 percent *condoned* such acts. In 1957, 80 percent of Americans thought it "neurotic" or "immoral" for a woman to remain unmarried by choice; by 1981, 75 percent not only believed that such action was appropriate, but also affirmed that it was acceptable for unmarried women to bear children. Only minorities of adults reported discomfort in 1981 "at having friends who were homosexuals." Apparently, the deeply moral America celebrated by observers ranging from de Tocqueville to Rostow had passed away in but a few short years.

Eloquent testimony on the moral revolution which this nation passed through comes from U.S. Senator Jeremiah Denton. As a Navy pilot, he was captured by the North Vietnamese in 1965 and spent the next eight years in isolation. When released in 1973, he returned to this country as a latter-day Rip Van Winkle, and experienced "shock" over the national landscape which he found: a land "of X-rated movies, massage parlors, the new [pornographic] literature on our newsstands, the degree to which our publishing industry had resorted to and favored books and magazines which were decidedly different from those I had seen before. . . ." He recently reiterated: "I am still shocked."[6]

From a shorter time perspective, Daniel P. Moynihan noted that the 1960s—a decade which "had begun with the utmost promise in America . . . would grow in strength and internal cohesion" and would likely achieve "a spirit of enterprise and daring such that history would look to it as a golden age"—had instead "progressed from vision to nightmare. The Great Republic had—incredibly, monstrously—been brought to the point of instability."[7]

Internal Weakness

What happened to "the American system" which had seemed so strong and vital during the 1950s? Simply put, it fell victim to both internal weaknesses and unprecedented ideological assault.

The former included:

(1) *The "Failure" of the Mainline Churches.* Despite an upsurge in church atendance during the 1950s, the American religious establishment began losing its nerve during the decade which followed. In particular, the "mainline" Protestant churches derived from the "nonconformist" heritage—Presbyterian, Congregationalist, and Methodist—proved unable to sustain any longer a theological justification for the American experiment. New bodies created in part to perform the task, such as the National Council of Churches of Christ, actually drifted into a particularly virulent form of opposition. In place of the orthodox emphasis on personal salvation and internalized morality, moreover, these churches turned to an altogether new non-judgmentalism concerning personal behavior. Accompanying this was a strange tendency to borrow "agendas" from secular political movements. In sum, the historic, Calvinist-based "faith" component of the American value consensus crumbled internally. Moreover, the other numerically significant religious groups found in America—Roman Catholic, Lutheran, Evangelical, Fundamentalist,

Mormon, and Jewish—proved either unwilling or unable to pick up the torch which had fallen.

(2) *The Race Question.* Minority groups, particularly blacks, were not wholly integrated into the American scheme. They were always the sociological exception, the national embarrassment. Marked by the heritage of slavery, Jim Crow, and racism, black families evidenced greater instability than their white counterparts. Moreover, popular celebrations of American identity during the 1950s—be they on television's situation comedies or in national magazines such as *Life* and *The Saturday Evening Post*—were characterized by a dearth of black, Hispanic, or Asiatic faces. While neither intrinsic nor necessary to the American system, this form of culturally-conditioned media racism left it vulnerable to criticism and attack.

And (3) *The Image of the "American Woman."* The commercialized media of the 1950s created an image of "the suburban American woman" committed to soap operas, "cleaner than clean" toilet bowls, and bridge clubs that was both sociologically misleading and psychologically inadequate. It proved susceptible to erosive and partly sound critiques such as Betty Friedan's 1963 book, *The Feminine Mystique.*

The Cultural War

Sensing the vulnerability of the American system, a whole range of ideological opponents then began their assault:

(1) *The Marxist Left.* The so-called "New Left" emerging during the 1960s revived the Marxist critique of the modern family as being based on male supremacy, property rights, and the perverse mythology of hearth and home. The family, these activists argued, should be viewed as merely another "functional prerequisite of capital" and motherhood as the means for the "reproduction of a future commodity of labor." As one self-styled American revolutionary wrote in 1971: "The insti-

tution of the family is inherently reactionary, and helps to maintain the capitalist system. The family ... is oppressive to its members. . . . Each nuclear family . . . weakens the class consciousness of the workers."[8] Inspired by Friedrich Engels, the New Left adopted old Marxist perspectives on "collective childrearing," "nonrepressive sexuality," and "oppressive motherhood" in pursuit of its agenda, correctly perceiving that market-capitalism and the American family model were closely related enemies.

(2) *The Sexual Libertarians.* The evidence reflecting major discontinuities in the erotic life of "the average American" after 1960 seems conclusive. By the early 1970s, most Americans—young and old alike—were having more sex, in different ways, with a greater variety of partners, and with less guilt afterwards than their counterparts from the late 1950s. Scientific developments such as oral contraceptives and the crumbling of traditional controls over youth sexuality both played a role in bringing on this change. But ideological forces were also at work. A new breed of "sex researchers," from Alfred Kinsey to Masters and Johnson, moved emphasis ever further away from viewing the sex act as an expression of human love toward preoccupation with the nature of the "physiological release" and the "health" of the sex organs.

More fundamentally, there were scattered individuals and groups actively working for the "obscening of America." In the Playboy Press' "official history" of the modern sex revolution, author Allan Sherman proved surprisingly candid. The sex revolution, he suggested, was led by "grown men and women, determined, dedicated and dirty-minded beyond the call of duty." He added:

Carefully, and often secretly, my generation manned (?) the battlefronts of the [Sex] Revolution. We produced and sold the rock 'n' roll records with risque lyrics; we invented the term 'wonder drug,' and LSD as the true panacea, pushing it at the kids in the hallowed atmosphere at Harvard. My generation wrote and read bestsellers with nothing more to recommend them than a half-dozen paragraphs of old-fashioned smut. . . . We invented or at least perfected wife-swapping. We performed illegal abortions. We crowded into the dark to watch those stupid stag films.[9]

According to Sherman, this conscious assault on the sexual restraints maintained by Western middle-class culture was soon transformed into an attack on the whole "incredibly clean-cut and impossibly wholesome" American world of Disney, church socials, Shirley Temple, the YMCA, Blondie and Dagwood, *The Saturday Evening Post,* motherhood, minature golf, apple pie, and hot dogs. In the end, Sherman suggested, the sex revolution of the 1960s and early '70s "removed America's backbone and revealed our awful secret: Stripped of the Puritan ethic, we have no morals at all." When it was over, he said, "we were coming unglued, splitting off into gaps and shards and lunatic fringes." Sherman added that "nothing was reduced to less recognizable rubble than the revered . . . Institution of Marriage."[10]

(3) *The Neo-Malthusians.* Fears of resource shortages and economic decline resulting from supposed American "over-population" began growing in the mid-1960s. The most fretful of the populationists soon turned from the advocacy of smaller families to open attacks on "the myth of Mom and Apple Pie" and the reproductive energies of the American family. Casting parenthood in a negative role, they argued for "micro" or "childfree" families to save the nation and world from disaster.[11]

(4) *The Radical Feminists.* The cutting edge of the emerging women's movement found the family—particularly children—to be an obstacle to its ideological goals. Kate Millet, for example, described society as an oppressive patriarchy. She cast women as "marginal citizens" and saw marriage as the place where a woman exchanged her sexuality for material support and confinement "in menial labor and compulsory

child-care."[12] Germaine Greer urged women to abandon their homes, husbands, and children in order to pursue their own needs and desires. If women were to achieve any change in their lives, "it seems obvious that they must refuse to marry." Abandoning one's children, she added, is "precisely the kind of brutally clear rethinking" that must take place.[13] The American home, a third feminist writer concluded, was "the basis of all evil."[14]

Other intellectual and social movements gleefully joined in the assault. Radical minority spokesmen attacked the "racist cultural imperialism" of the white middle class for imposing its supposedly alien family norms and morality on blacks, Hispanics, and Native Americans. Homosexuals blasted the exalted status given to the family, hoping to end such special treatment and win acceptance of their "sexual orientation" as merely another life-style. And so on through the list.

The State vs. the Family

The U.S. government itself absorbed elements of these ideologies and—in what can only be described as a semi-conscious effort at national suicide—began randomly attacking the once celebrated American system.

Neo-Malthusianism, for example, began winning official sanction. In 1965, President Lyndon Johnson convened a White House Conference on International Cooperation that included a Panel on Population. In the words of panel member John D. Rockefeller III, "population stabilization" must be considered "a necessary means to the enhancement and enrichment of human life."[15] Johnson appointed in 1968 a President's Committee on Population and Family Planning, which urged a greater federal presence in the population control area. A year later, in an unprecedented Message to Congress on Population, President Richard Nixon called on all Americans to respond rapidly to "the population crisis" facing the nation and world. He urged that "the United

Nations, its specialized agencies and other international bodies should take the lead in responding to world population growth. . . ."[16] Congress subsequently created a Commission on Population Growth and the American Future, "to formulate policy" dealing with "the pervasive impact of population growth on every facet of American life." Its 1972 report declared that the United States should "welcome and plan for stabilized population" through a comprehensive program of fertility and population control and sex education. Specific recommendations included federal efforts to make abortion, sterilization, and contraceptive services available to all Americans (including minors without the consent of their parents), and new federal programs "to support the development of a variety of model programs in human sexuality."[17] Large and moderately sized families as well as sexual restraint—viewed in the 1950s as signs of robust national health—had become virtual social pathologies and the targets of state activism by the early 1970s.

Policy consequences were soon rolling in. The 1972 Family Planning Act reflected pervasive Malthusian influence. For the first time, it moved the awesome power of the federal government into the family and sexual arenas by providing federal subsidization for birth control clinics. Federal funds also began flowing into "population education" curricula, which filled children with fear over the horrors of too many offspring and trumpeted the beauties of "childfree" relationships. Assaults on such "pronatalist" incentives as the personal income tax exemption also helped justify the progressive erosion of the exemption's value. In consequence, between 1960 and 1984, the federal income tax burden shifted dramatically onto the backs of families with dependent children. According to one recent study, single persons and married couples without children face essentially the same average tax rate in 1984 as their married counterparts did 25 years before. However, a family with two children confronts an increase of 43 percent in its average tax rate, while a couple with four children faces a staggering rise of 223 percent![18]

The government also succumbed to the anti-family attitudes beginning to dominate sociology, psychology, and the other "social sciences." During the 1950s, sociologist Talcott Parsons and his colleagues at Harvard University had guided the bulk of that profession into a celebration of the American experiment, focused in particular on the nation's strong family norms and pervasive religiousity. Starting in the mid-1960s, though, social scientists turned on the family with an inexplicable bitterness. In an altogether characteristic article, anthropologist Ray Birdwhistell described men, women, and children inside their suburban homes as "cage dependent." Marriage counselors, social workers, psychiatrists, and family doctors who accepted the American family model as "healthy," he continued, were no better than "zoo keepers" sustaining a gross pathology. Birdwhistell specifically objected to both "... the fantastic notion that one man and one woman should mate and after that be responsible for satisfying all of the other's significant emotional needs" and "the other equally exotic and impossible . . . idea that parents should be responsible for meeting all their children's needs." In a subsequent article, Birdwhistell demanded the destruction of "this impossibly overloaded and guilt-creating social unit, the family."[19]

Such ideas quickly found a federal platform. Forum 14 of the 1970 White House Conference on Children and Youth blasted American society's past conformity and welcomed the emerging movement "to destroy the cultural myth of a 'right' or 'best' way to behave, believe, work, or play." Composed of a cross-section of the nation's most well-connected "family scholars," the Forum celebrated a newly "pluralistic society of varying family forms and a multiplicity of cultures." Defining family as "a group of individuals in interaction," the family experts described optional forms ranging from "nuclear families" to "single parent," "communal," "group marriage," and "homosexual" varieties. Audaciously ignoring the needs of children, the Forum went on to urge active government support for "the right of individuals to live in any family form they feel will increase their options for self-fulfillment."[20]

The reputed family experts also began sweeping aside mounting evidence of family disruption and resulting human pain with the glib retort that "families aren't collapsing, they're changing." Serving as major institutional stimulants to this theme were the 1971 and 1972 sessions of the Groves Conference on Marriage and the Family. The gloom and uncertainty found at such meetings in the late 1960s gave way to an orgy of intellectual excitement over "the varied family forms phenomenon." By the mid-1970s, according to one survey, over 80 percent of the nation's rank-and-file marriage and family counselors had accepted "... co-marital sex (CMS) and alternative / experimental / emerging / variant / innovative / non-traditional marriage forms" as normal, even healthy "options."[21] By extending the definition of "family" to cover virtually every conceivable form of human contact, the professionals had indeed turned human tragedy and professional failure into seeming triumph. A great lie had been born.

But when Jimmy Carter, a man of some native common sense, came along during his 1976 Presidential campaign and declared that "the American family is in trouble" and—as President—issued a call for a White House Conference on *The American Family,* the whole charade was threatened. Once handed over to the Department of Health, Education, and Welfare bureaucrats, though, the "family conference" concept was captured by the family professionals. Within months, the event was relabeled The White House Conference *on Families.* "Pluralism" and "changing families" displaced "the family is in trouble" as the organizing theme. As Chairperson Jim Guy Tucker emphasized in his welcoming comments to the conference's advisory committee, "we're going to focus on the realities of today's families, their diversity and pluralism."[22] Scholars participating in the White House Conference's 1980 Research Forum concluded that "what we are witnessing today is not the breakup of the traditional family pattern but the emergence of a pluralism in family ways."[23] The Lie's Triumph at the heart of the government was complete.

America's Great Schism

So where are we left? Instead of the "open society" promised by the partisans of the "new pluralism," our population today is deeply divided. According to social pollster Daniel Yankelovich, about one-fifth of Americans strongly adhere to the traditional values of family, religious faith, hard work, and self-denial. Another fifth have adapted what he calls the values of "self-actualization," generally meaning a rejection of transcendent morality, an avoidance of familial responsibility, and the discarding of socially-regulated sexual inhibition. The remaining 60 percent, he suggests, drift somewhere in-between. Indeed, bitter differences over abortion, school prayer, children's rights, "family protection," sex education, and other "social issues" reflect unprecedented divisions within the population, a fundamental conflict of world views. In light of this, Yankelovich expects American culture to be "a cockpit of conflict" for the remainder of the century as these fissures work themselves out.[24] Philosopher Alasdair MacIntyre goes further, describing contemporary American politics as "civil war carried out by other means."[25] In the moral vacuum which the "abortion ethic" has created, our nation's own mountain of tiny corpses—all conveniently dehumanized as "fetal matter"—continues to grow. The ghosts of interwar France and Germany loom large across the American landscape.

In the face of this situation, what can morally sensitive Americans do? To begin with, and however heated the cultural and political wars become, dialogue and civility must be maintained. It is here that the organized churches have their crucial role: not as institutional partisans on one or another barricade, but as healers, reconcilers, politically neutral forums, and the places where combatants may confess their common sin and seek God's saving grace.

For individuals committed to the Judeo-Christian moral order, the long term cultural goal must be the restoration of the vital center in America: the re-creation of a core of common values around which the large majority of the citizenry can again rally. I believe that this new "center" will, of necessity, greatly resemble the "old" consensus built around family and faith, albeit purged of the weaknesses described earlier. For I think those observers are wrong who suggest that a wholly new vision of moral community can be conjured out of thin air. Rather, the whole of human experience testifies that successful moral community must be deeply rooted in history, religious humility, and the exercise of social responsibility.

The task of re-creation is complex and enormous. It involves basic changes in the whole array of culture-shaping activities: literature, art, the print and electronic media, the schools, and institutional religion itself. Nonetheless, the future that our children will inhabit and the kind of people that they shall be are both at stake.

A Policy Agenda

Politics stands secondary to these critical cultural tasks. But within the political realm, there are three interim steps that seem both necessary and appropriate.

First, neo-Malthusianism's ideological hammerlock on the federal government should be broken. Individual use of artificial birth control is not and should not be treated as the issue. Rather, argument should focus on the fundamental errors lying behind the neo-Malthusian ideological system. The Rev. Thomas Malthus was wholly wrong in the 1790s when he attributed poverty and hunger to population pressure. The neo-Malthusians are equally wrong today when they blame hunger, poverty, and environmental stress on human numbers.[26] The real blame, then as now, falls on governments and cultures which block innovation, movement, and growth, and on human avarice and greed, which exist even in a population of two. Neo-Malthusian doctrine—which in our day has taken on a twisted anti-family, anti-human gloss—has spread throughout the governmental apparatus, justifying everything from "abortion on demand" at home to the U.S.-funded promotion of sterilization procedures abroad; from massive sex education efforts in the public schools to a tax policy which punishes young couples foolish enough to challenge the spirit of the age and actually bear children.

A specific political agenda aimed at ending the hegemony of the Malthusians would include: (1) repeal of the Family Planning Act, thus ending a process whereby federally funded agencies place themselves between parent and child on the most fundamental questions; (2) an end to all federal subsidization of "sex education" curricula and "population education" programs; and (3) the cessation of federal funding for population control work overseas by the U.S. Agency for International Development and the United Nations.

Second, federal tax policy deserves special attention. The massive shift of the income tax burden onto families with children since 1960 is both an extreme form of anti-family social policy and exceedingly poor tax policy. A theoretically easy response would be to raise the value of the personal exemption to its original level. Yet in order to offset the same percentage of *per capita* income in 1984 as it did in 1948, the exemption would need to rise from its current level of $1000 to $5600. Given current budgetary pressures, this figure is unrealistic. An alternative and more practical solution, proposed by Treasury analyst Eugene Steuerle, is to create a new tax rate schedule for couples with dependents where brackets would be at least twice as wide as those applying to single persons. This course would have the additional advantage of eliminating the notorious "marriage penalty" for two-income couples with children.[27]

Finally, educational policy needs to be addressed. Learning

cannot proceed in a moral vacuum. And indeed, until America's "great schism" after 1960, public education remained grounded in the fundamentally religious, historically "American" virtues laid out by Horace Mann in the 1840s: "... piety, justice, and a sacred regard to truth, love to . . . country, humanity, and universal benevolence, sobriety, industry, and frugality, chastity, moderation, and temperance, and those other virtues . . . upon which a republican constitution is found."[28]

Today, I think it safe to conclude that these virtues no longer form the backbone of American public education. Instead, we are witnesses to the corruption and decay of the state school system. Like France's government-paid educators during the 1920s, an apparent majority of our public school teachers have become politicized and have cast their lot with the politics of the Left. Also reflecting the earlier French experience, Christian and Jewish parents are pulling massive numbers of their children out of the public system and expanding or creating their own religiously grounded "free" schools.

Moreover, as our sense of national community has broken down, the controversies surrounding public education have mounted, creating new dilemmas. "In a society *as incredibly diverse* as late twentieth-century America," educator Lucy Patterson suggests, "the only way we can all live at peace with one another is to take volatile issues like feminism, sex education, and creationism out of the 'winner take all' arena of monopoly education." Unless minority moral communities have the option to send children to schools consistent with their beliefs, she argues, "the politics of public education will keep growing harsher, shriller, and more depressing."[29]

Creating "communities of virtues" is at present beyond the capability of the public schools. Indeed, programs such as "values clarification" and sex education, when torn away from objective morality, have tended to turn the state schools into prime engines for national disintegration, encouraging through an absolute value relativism a cynicism toward social morality altogether. In contrast, private schools still enjoy freedom from most externally imposed legal, structural, and ideological restraints and freedom for the creation of moral codes evoking the shared commitments of the community involved.

Until the cultural resources have been mobilized to rebuild a new consensus on values, it is imperative that public policy foster such small centers of freedom and virtue. A combination of tuition tax credits and educational vouchers would give all elements of the population, not just the relatively wealthy, access to choice and moral community in their children's education. A federal income tax credit for a portion of tuition paid to private schools would aid middle-income families. Title I of the Elementary and Secondary Education Act of 1965, which currently provides categorical aid for the education of disadvantaged children, could be restructured to parcel out the funds (in the form of a voucher) directly to the parents of such children. Each family would then be free to use its voucher at the public or private school of its choice. If such a scheme proved successful, state funding mechanisms could also be restructured to create a universal voucher plan within each state.

These are small steps designed to help preserve the possibility for renewal of national community in the future. Dangerous divisions exist in our society. Moral relativism and social alienation have spread deep. For the believer, though, hope and charity serve to banish the spectres of fear and despair. With God's grace, the courage that derives from faith shall animate those who begin to mount the effort.

FIVE

Abortion: The Judeo-Christian Imperative

W. Douglas Badger

IN 1981, A 40-YEAR-OLD WOMAN, pregnant for the first time, underwent amniocentesis to determine whether her un-born child was "defective." In the wake of legalized abortion, amniocentesis, a test used to identify the handicapped before birth so that they can be aborted, has become commonplace. The results in this instance were not. Physicians told the woman that she was carrying a Downs syndrome child—and a normal one.

"The mother desperately wanted to have the normal child but could not face the burden of caring for the handicapped one for the rest of her life," said Dr. Thomas Kerenyi, clinical professor of obstetrics at New York's Mt. Sinai School of Medicine.[1] Dr. Kerenyi and his associate, Dr. Usha Chitkara, proposed a solution to the woman's dilemma which broke new technological ground, at least in the United States. Their solution: "selective birth."

"We were mainly concerned about performing it without inadvertently bringing harm to the normal fetus," Kerenyi and

Chitkara explained in the June 18, 1981, issue of the *New England Journal of Medicine.* "We realized that this was more important than the fate of the affected twin, and that acceptance of this procedure in the future would hinge on the outcome of the normal, unaffected twin."[2] Standard second trimester abortion techniques are not sufficiently refined to make such distinctions. They would kill both babies. So the doctors resorted to a procedure which had been used once before in Sweden. They pierced the heart of the Down's syndrome child with a hollow needle and aspirated half his blood supply.

"The needle had to hit a moving target less than an inch across," the *New York Times* reported, "and there was a risk of killing both fetuses, damaging the abnormal one without killing it, or even killing the normal one by mistake."[3] Kerenyi and Chitkara were not certain until the woman delivered a healthy baby and his stillborn brother that they had achieved their "pro-choice" milestone. For this was not an abortion in the usual sense of the term. It did not relieve the woman of an unplanned pregnancy. She had chosen to become pregnant and to carry her pregnancy to term. She had also chosen to give birth to one son and to have the other killed. The doctors executed her choice with precision.

Abortion as the Killing of Human Beings

What is more, *The New York Times* described this "selective birth" with precision. In a striking choice of words for a newspaper with a staunchly pro-abortion editorial policy, the *Times* thrice characterized the procedure as "killing." Abortion proponents ordinarily avoid the word "kill" when writing about abortion and sharply criticize pro-lifers for refusing to observe the same protocol. Essayist Joseph Sobran once observed that the word "kill" was used only twice in Planned Parenthood's *Handbook on Abortion*:

once to mention how pregnant women used to kill themselves in the dark ages before the Supreme Court spoke and
again in describing the operation of contraceptives to kill
sperm... You can kill yourself, you see, and you can kill a
little tiny sperm; you can kill an elephant, and you can kill a
bacterium; we even speak of killing cancerous cells. But you
can't kill a fetus. You can only "terminate (a pregnancy)."[4]

This refusal to concede that abortion involves the killing of
human beings is entirely self-conscious. Abortion advocate
Malcolm Potts, in a 1970 *California Medicine* editorial, said
that it is essential to the pro-abortion strategy to:

separate the idea of abortion from the idea of killing, which
continues to be socially abhorrent. The result has been the
curious avoidance of the scientific fact, which everyone
really knows, that human life begins at conception and is
continuous whether intra- or extra-uterine until death. The
very considerable semantic gymnastics which are required
to rationalize abortion as anything but taking a human life
would be ludicrous if they were not often put forth under
socially impeccable auspices.[5]

Unborn children are human beings. That, as Dr. Potts
observes, is a "scientific fact, which everyone really knows."
But it is a fact that must be suppressed in the service of the
pro-abortion agenda. It has become increasingly difficult to
suppress in the years that have passed since the publication of
Dr. Potts' editorial. Today, for example, clinics throughout
the United States specialize in *in vitro* fertilization. Practi-
tioners of this technique remove a woman's ovum, fertilize it
in a petri dish with her husband's sperm, and then incubate it
for 7 to 10 days—hence the popular term "test tube babies"—
before implanting the tiny embryo in the mother's womb. The
mother delivers her baby after the normal gestation period.

This technique could never have succeeded unless two assumptions were scientifically correct: 1) that a unique human life comes into existence at conception; and 2) that this life can exist independently of his or her mother's body even in the earliest days of life.

The humanity of the unborn is also evident to surgeons who now can operate on some babies while they are yet in their mother's wombs. Fr. Richard McCormick of Georgetown University says of fetal surgery, "Already I hear the doctors involved in this refer to the fetus as their patient. The fetus now begins to make serious claims for a right to nutrition, to protection, to therapy. How can tolerance of abortion be morally reconciled with those claims?"[6]

Discarding the Judeo-Christian Ethic

Tolerance of abortion cannot be morally reconciled with the Judeo-Christian view of human life. For that reason, Potts says, the Judeo-Christian view must be swept away by a new ethic. Social acceptance of abortion is at the vanguard of that new ethic. In the future, Potts says:

It will become necessary and acceptable to place relative rather than absolute values on such things as human lives.... This is quite distinctly at variance with the Judeo-Christian ethic and carries serious philosophical, social, economic and political implications for Western society and perhaps for world society.[7]

The Judeo-Christian ethic, Potts says, is giving way to the new ethic because acceptance of abortion is coming to permeate the law and the churches.

The process of eroding the old ethic and substituting the new has already begun. It may be seen most clearly in changing attitues toward human abortion. In defiance of the long held Western ethic of intrinsic and equal values for every human life regardless of its stage, condition or status, abortion is becoming accepted by society as moral, right and even necessary. It is worth noting that this shift in public attitude has affected the churches, the laws and public policy rather than the reverse.[8]

This shift in values, Potts believes, is only the beginning. If society can tolerate the destruction of unborn human beings, it will come to tolerate the destruction of other classes of human beings as well.

Medicine's role with respect to changing attitudes toward abortion may well be a prototype of what is to occur... One may anticipate further development of these roles as the problems of birth control and birth selection are extended inevitably to death selection and death control whether by the individual or by society.[9]

Potts thus foresees an inexorable advance from private choice of abortion to societal death selection—legalized and publicly regulated euthanasia. But to begin this advance, the wall of Judeo-Christian values must first be breached. And it will be breached, he argues, when abortion is broadly accepted by secularists and Christians alike.

Australian bioethicist Dr. Peter Singer, who, like Potts, advocates abortion, also believes that broad acceptance of abortion portends the death of the Judeo-Christian ethic. Writing in support of infanticide in the July, 1983, issue of *Pediatrics,* Singer argues that the "quality of life ethic" is eclipsing the "sanctity of life ethic."

The first major blow to the sanctity of life view was the spreading acceptance of abortion throughout the Western world. ... A second blow to the sanctity of life view has been the revelation that it is standard practice in many major public hospitals to refrain from providing necessary life-saving treatment to certain patients.... In Britain, Dr. John Lorber has quite candidly described his method of selecting which babies suffering from spina bifida should be given active treatment, and he has indicated, with equal candor, that in his view the best possible outcome for those not selected is an early death.[10]

Singer welcomes these developments. Society must abandon the sanctity of life view, he argues, because it is no longer tenable.

We can no longer base our ethics on the idea that human beings are a special form of creation, made in the image of God, singled out from all other animals, and alone possessing an immortal soul.... Once the religious mumbo-jumbo has been stripped away, we may continue to see normal members of our species as possessing greater capacities of rationality, self-consciousness, communication, and so on, than members of any other species; but we will not regard as sacrosanct the life of each and every member of our species.... If we compare a severely defective human infant with a nonhuman animal, a dog or a pig, for example, we will often find the nonhuman to have superior capacities, both actual and potential, for ... anything that can plausibly be considered morally significant. Only the fact that the defective infant is a member of the species *Homo sapiens* leads it to be treated differently from the dog or pig. Species membership alone, however, is not morally relevant.[11]

Notice that neither Potts nor Signer dispute the humanity of the unborn child. Both are quite willing to concede that. For Potts, the unborn's humanity is "a scientific fact, which everyone really knows"—a fact to be evaded in public discourse, but one that does not diminish his enthusiasm for abortion. For Singer, the unborn child is indeed a living "member of the species *Homo sapiens,*" but that is not "relevant" to a consideration of the morality of abortion or infanticide. The abortion debate, both men will attest, is not a conflict over when life begins, but a conflict between two views of human life. The Judeo-Christian tradition, characterized by Singer as a belief in the sanctity of life, regards each person as valuable because each person bears God's image. Since the unborn child is a living human being—a member of the species *Homo sapiens*—his or her life has value. The quality of life ethic regards human beings as valuable only if society thinks them valuable. Severely handicapped newborns are not valuable. Nor are unwanted fetuses. The law should therefore be indifferent to their destruction.

American law has become increasingly indifferent to the destruction of the unborn. The Supreme Court substantially aided this process in 1973 with its now infamous *Roe* v. *Wade* decision. In that case, the Court discovered that the right of privacy "is broad enough to encompass a woman's decision whether or not to terminate her pregnancy."[12] Writing for the majority, Justice Harry Blackmun upended one of the pillars of the sanctity of life ethic, the Oath of Hippocrates. Blackmun dismissed the Oath, which explicitly forbids abortion, as "a Pythagorean manifesto and not the expression of an absolute standard of medical conduct."[13] The Judeo-Christian resistance to abortion represented for Blackmun a peculiar dogma, one to which "ancient religion"—pre-Christian paganism— did not adhere.[14]

As to the humanity of unborn children, the Court maintained a learned ignorance.

> We need not resolve the difficult question of when life begins. When those trained in the respective disciplines of medicine, philosophy and theology are unable to arrive at any consensus, the judiciary, at this point in the development of man's knowledge, is not in a position to speculate as to the answer.[15]

That difficult question, as Dr. Potts observed, has been affirmatively answered, not by theologians or philosophers, but by scientists. On this point, Blackmun was engaged in semantic gymnastics, obviously desiring a result (permissive abortion) more than either philosophical or moral clarity.

Since the judiciary could not ascertain whether fetuses are human beings, Blackmun concluded that restrictions on abortion rest on "one theory of life," a constitutionally infirm theory since such restrictions encroach on a woman's right of privacy.[16] Blackmun accorded unborn children no constitutional status. They are not, in his view, "persons in the whole sense."[17]

Since unborn children have no rights, the court did not have to balance the rights of a woman against those of her child. Instead, it weighed the expectant mother's right of privacy against the state's interest in regulating that right.[18] The state's interest, the Court concluded, weighed almost nothing at all. Its ruling effectively nullified the abortion laws of all fifty states. It made abortion, as a matter of constitutional law, legally permissible throughout pregnancy. As the Court put it:

(a) For the stage prior to approximately the end of the first trimester, the abortion decision and its effectuation must be left to the medical judgment of the pregnant woman's attending physician.

(b) For the stage subsequent to approximately the end of the first trimester, the State, in promoting its interest in the health of the mother, may, if it chooses, regulate the abortion procedure in ways that are reasonably related to maternal health.

(c) For the stage subsequent to viability [the Court reckoned that the unborn child became viable at approximately 24-28 weeks gestation], the State in promoting its interest in the potentiality of human life may, if it chooses, regulate, and even proscribe, abortion except where it is necessary, in appropriate medical judgment, for the preservation of the life or health of the mother.[19]

In a companion decision, the Court defined "health of the mother" as embracing "*all* the attending circumstances," including "physical, emotional, psychological, familial and the woman's age."[20]

Justice Byron White captured the decision's essence when he wrote in his dissent:

For any one of such reasons, or for no reason at all, and without asserting or claiming any threat to life or health, any woman is entitled to an abortion if she is able to find a medical advisor willing to undertake the procedure.[21]

Roe v. *Wade,* Justice White correctly observed, requires that abortion be legally available on demand throughout the entire course of pregnancy. "The Court apparently values the convenience of the pregnant mother more than the continued existence and development of the life or potential life that she carries," he wrote. "Whether or not I might agree with that marshalling of values . . . I find no warrant for imposing such an order of priorities on the people."[22]

White recognized something that the majority of his brethren did not: *Roe* v. *Wade* was *not* a neutral decision. Rather, *Roe* enshrined a controversial view of the nature of unborn human life under the sacred canopy of the Constitution, and *ipso facto* excluded all competing views. Under its terms, a woman's right to destroy her baby is constitutionally protected; an unborn child's right to live is not, nor *may* it be protected by state statute. Put another way, *Roe* v. *Wade* made the quality of life ethic, at least as it pertains to abortion, the law of the land.

The Testimony of Science

The Court's edict in *Roe* v. *Wade* is not ordinarily understood as establishing a federal position on the value of human life, much less as preferring one view of life over another. Indeed, Blackmun believed that he had seized the high ground of neutrality when he forbade states from using antiabortion laws to "elevate one theory of life above all others."[23] Blackmun perceived the abortion debate as a clash between those who dogmatically insist that human life begins at conception and those who regard life's beginning as an impenetrable mystery. To leave the abortion decision to each individual appeared to him as a way not to take sides. Those who believe fetuses to be human need not procure abortions; those who believe that they are not, or that they become human at some advanced stage of pregnancy, are free to obtain abortions safely and legally.

But the question of when life begins is not, as we have seen, inscrutable. It is, in abortion advocate Malcolm Potts' words, a "scientific fact, which everyone really knows, that human life begins at conception." To treat that fact as an unproven proposition is therefore ludicrous, like maintaining no position on the shape of the earth or the laws of gravity. To withdraw the law's protection from human beings in the womb, which is what the Court did, is thus to elevate one theory of life—the quality of life theory—above all others. A Senate Judiciary subcommittee, which heard from a succession of world-renowned scientists in 1981, drew this very conclusion.

"In biology and in medicine," Harvard medical school professor Micheline Mathews-Roth told the panel, "it is an accepted fact that the life of any individual organism reproducing by sexual reproduction begins at conception. . . . No experiments have disproved this finding. So it is scientifically correct to say that an individual life begins at conception . . . and that this developing human always is a member of our species in all stages of its life."[24]

"[This] is the first time I have found myself having to argue the inarguable," Mayo Clinic geneticist Hymie Gordon testified. "I have never encountered in my reading—long before I became concerned with abortion, euthanasia and so on—anyone who has argued that life did not begin at the moment of conception. . . . There has been no argument about these matters."[25]

Internationally renowned geneticist Jerome Lejeune of Paris said, "There is no new revelation we have done in front of you—just telling you what is taught in every genetics course in every country. . . . When people say this has metaphysical connotations they are perfectly correct. . . . But the scientific fact that it is a human being cannot be disputed."[26]

Dr. Hymie Gordon added, "We can say unequivocally that the question of when life begins is no longer a question for theological or philosophical dispute. Theologians and philosophers may go on to debate the meaning of life or the purpose of life, but it is an established fact that all life, including human life, begins at the moment of conception."[27]

Pro-abortion scientists who appeared before the committee, significantly, did not directly refute the testimony of those who had gone before them. Indeed, they could not have, for to do so would have been to refute, as Professor Lejeune said, "what is taught in every genetics course in every country."

Instead, when confronted with the question, "When does science say that human life begins?" the scientists went into a semantic gymnastics routine. "We won't answer that question because the answer is irrelevant to your political judgment," some, in effect, said. (The committee had solicited testimony because it was considering proposed legislation to reverse *Roe* v. *Wade.*) Others said that the abortion issue cannot be resolved by science.

That is true enough. The issue of whether human life should be legally protected is not one for scientists but for policy makers. But the question of whether unborn children are human beings is answerable by science. The subcommittee made this critical distinction in its report.

> We must consider not only whether unborn children are human beings but also whether to accord their lives intrinsic worth and value equal to other human beings. The two questions are separate and distinct. It is a scientific question whether an unborn child is a human being... It is a value question whether the life of an unborn child has intrinsic worth and equal value with other human beings.[28]

Having drawn that distinction, the report closely scrutinized the testimony of scientists who declined to answer the question of when human life begins.

> These witnesses who testified that science cannot say whether unborn children are human beings were speaking in every instance to the value question rather than the scientific question. No witness raised any evidence to refute the biological fact that from the moment of human conception there exists a distinct individual being who is alive and is of the human species. ...
>
> Disregarding the customary scientific definition of human being, some witnesses sought to make "human being" and "humanness" into undefined concepts that vary according to one's values. They took the view that each person may define as "human" only those beings whose lives that person wants to value. Because they did not wish to accord intrinsic worth to the lives of unborn children, they refused to call them "human beings."[29]

Thus, the only federal panel ever to examine the scientific question of when life begins has concluded that the abortion debate does not involve a dispute over facts, but a dispute over values. The most important fact, the committee said, is beyond cavil: abortion kills living human beings. No one who cares to discuss the issue honestly can deny that fact. For those who subscribe to the sanctity of life ethic, that fact completes the syllogism—all human beings have intrinsic worth and deserve legal protection, unborn children are human beings, therefore unborn children have intrinsic worth and deserve legal protection.

For those who subscribe to the quality of life ethic, matters are not so simple. To say that unborn children are human beings is not to say that they have value. "Species membership alone," Singer says, "is not morally relevant." For advocates of such a view, unborn children have no value if their mothers do not want them. Abortion must be permitted even though it is killing; of course, public relations considerations usually prohibit so blunt a statement of the "pro-choice" position. Yet, though the abortion advocates profess not to know whether the unborn are human beings, their sophist tactics cannot still the voice of science.

What an Abortion Is

Nor can they still the voice of their own consciences. At the 1978 meeting of the Association of Planned Parenthood Physicians, Dr. Warren M. Hern and Billie Corrigan, a registered nurse, presented a paper entitled "What About Us?" an exploration of the "medical and emotional sequelae" of second trimester abortion performed by the dilatation and extraction (D & E) method.[30] This technique is fast becoming the procedure of choice for midtrimester abortions, particularly in the wake of the Supreme Court's "Akron Ordinance" decision in June, 1983, which prohibited states from requiring that second trimester abortions be done in hospitals.[31] D & E, unlike other methods commonly used in the second trimester, can safely be done in abortion clinics.

The procedure is brutal and direct. The physician dilates the mother's cervix, much as he would in performance of a first trimester abortion. Monographs specify the use of 14mm

forceps with no-slip transverse ridges to complete the procedure. This is described in a second article by Sadja Goldsmith.
"The fetus was extracted in small pieces to minimize cervical
trauma. The fetal head was often the most difficult object to
crush because of its size and contour. The operator kept track
of each portion of the fetal skeleton in order to be sure of
complete evacuation."[32]

The task of fetal reconstruction in the operating room,
designed to ensure the success of the abortion, is the
assignment of the attending nurse. It is the trauma of this
activity that is the object of the Hern-Corrigan paper, for the
"medical and emotional sequelae" in this study of abortion are
not those experienced by the patient but those of the doctor
and the staff who assist him.

The sequelae, Hern and Corrigan learned through inter-
views with more than a dozen medical staff who had participated in the procedure, are profound.

> Two respondents described dreams which they had had
> related to the procedure. Both described dreams of vomit-
> ing fetuses along with a sense of horror. Other dreams
> revolved around a need to protect others from viewing fetal
> parts, dreaming that she herself was pregnant and needed an
> abortion or was having a baby.[33]

Hern and Corrigan do not understand this intrusion of
conscience into their dreams, although that is clearly what is
taking place. "No one who has not performed this procedure
can know what it is like or what it means," they write, "but
having performed it, we are bewildered by the possibilities of
interpretation. We have reached a point in this particular
technology where there is no possibility of denial of an act of
destruction by the operator. It is before one's eyes. The
sensations of dismemberment flow through the forceps like an
electric current."[34]

Dr. William Benbow Thompson of the University of

California at Irvine made a similar observation. "You are doing a destructive process," he said, "Arms, legs, chests come out in the forceps. It's not a sight for everybody."[35]

"Remember," said Dr. Julius Butler, a professor of obstetrics and gynecology at the University of Minnesota Medical School, "there is a human being at the other end of the table taking that kid apart."[36] However, it is the abortionist's humanity, not his victim's, that Butler feels constrained to defend.

The point in examining those closest to the actual performance of abortions is not simply to shock the reader, although this is perhaps inevitable. Rather, the intention is to take abortion out of the realm of politics or abstract argument and to focus instead on the undeniable reality of precisely what an abortion is. Examination of abortion techniques, rather than philosophical niceties, is a sobering but necessary exercise.

Dr. Magda Denes, an advocate of abortion who has had one herself, has inadvertently done pro-lifers a great service by providing detailed description of day-to-day life in an abortion hospital. It is not a pleasant picture. After observing the abortion of one 17-year-old girl, whom she gave the pseudonym, Catherine Atkins, Denes went to a room in the hospital where aborted babies were stored in "paper buckets"—as she puts it, "the type in which one buys fried chicken from take-home stores."[38]

> I look inside the bucket in front of me. There is a small naked person in there floating in a bloody liquid—plainly the tragic victim of a drowning accident. But then perhaps this was no accident, because the body is purple with bruises and the face has the agonized tautness of one forced to die too soon. Death overtakes me in a rush . . .
>
> I take the lid off all the buckets. All of them. I reach up to the shelf above this bucket graveyard tabletop and take down a pair of forceps. With them I pull aside in each bucket the placenta . . . With the forceps I lift the fetuses, one by

one. I lift them by an arm or a leg, leaving, as I return them again, an additional bruise on their purple, wrinkled, acid-soaked flesh. I have evidently gone mad. Finally, I lift a very large fetus whose position is such that, rather than its face, I first see its swollen testicles . . . Mother's name: Catherine Atkins . . .

I remember Catherine. She is seventeen, a very pretty blond girl. Not very bright. This is Master Atkins—to be burned tomorrow—who died like a hero to save his mother's life. Might he have become someday the only one to truly love her? The only one to mourn her death?

"Nurse, nurse," I shout, taking off my fancy gloves. "Cover them up."[39]

But abortion's victims are not so easily covered up. Their lives are extinguished in a moment; their memory is not. Neither the rhetoric that dehumanizes the unborn nor the fiction that abortionists serve as agents of women's reproductive rights can silence the abortionist's conscience. Every abortionist knows that he earns his living as a practitioner of violence. "We'll just have to face it," one abortionist told Denes. "Somebody has to do it. And, unfortunately, we are the executioners in this instance."[40]

Women who have undergone abortion know this torment. Nancy Jo Mann, founder of Women Exploited by Abortion, is one such woman. She gives this account of her abortion.

I went in and I asked, "What are you going to do to me?" All he (the physician) did was look at my stomach and say, "I'm going to take a little fluid out, put a little fluid in, you'll have severe cramps and expel the fetus."

I said, "Is that all?" He said, "That's all." It did not sound too bad. But what the doctor described to me was not the truth.

Once they put in the saline, there's no way to reverse it. And for the next hour and a half I felt my daughter thrash around violently while she was being choked, poisoned, burned, and suffocated to death. I didn't know any of that was going to happen. And I remember talking to her and I remember telling her I didn't want to do this, I wished she could live. And yet she was dying and I remember her very last kick on her left side. She had no strength left. I've tried to imagine that kind of death, a pillow put over us, suffocating. In four minutes we'd pass out. We'd have that gift of passing out and then dying. But it took her an hour and half just to die.

Then I was given an intravenous injection to help stimulate labor for 12 hours. And at 5:30 AM on the 31st day of October I delivered my daughter, whose name is now Charmaine Marie. She was 14 inches long. She weighed over a pound and a half. She had a head of hair and her eyes were opening.

I got to hold her because the nurses didn't make it to the room in time. I delivered the girl myself. They grabbed her out of my hands and threw her, threw her, into a bedpan.[41]

Mann learned painfully what her abortionists already knew: to participate in an abortion is to participate in the destruction of another's life. She has dedicated her life to seeing that as many women as possible can be spared the same tragedy. Many who acknowledge the destructive reality of abortion, however, nevertheless believe abortion to be a tragic necessity, one that the law must permit. The *New Republic* has taken this position.

Those who believe a woman should be free to have an abortion must face the consequences of their beliefs. Metaphysical arguments about the beginning of life are fruitless. But there clearly is no logical or moral distinction between a fetus and a young baby; free availability of abortion cannot be reasonably distinguished from infanticide ...

Nevertheless, we are for it. It is too facile to say that

human life is always sacred; obviously it is not, and the social cost of preserving against the mother's will the lives of fetuses who are not yet self-conscious is simply too great.[42]

Human life "obviously" is not always sacred. Society must resign itself to 1.5 million abortions each year because the "social cost" of protecting unborn human beings is "simply too great." That is the quality of life mentality which has so insidiously and pervasively gripped our public policy in the preceding decade.

The Judeo-Christian Imperative

The Judeo-Christian understanding of human life, as Potts and Singer and others have recognized, is quite different. The scriptures teach that each human life is sacred, that life is a gift of the living God. In contrast to the Gentile nations who manufacture gods in their image, Yahweh fashions human beings in his image (Gn 1:26-28). Each person thus is vested with an inviolable dignity on the basis of his or her creation.

The scriptures also reveal that God is the protector of life, as well as its creator. After the Fall, Cain considers killing his brother. Before Cain resolves to commit murder, God intervenes. "Why are you angry? Why is your face downcast?" God asks Cain. "If you do what is right, will you not be accepted? But if you do not do what is right, sin is crouching at your door; it desires to have you, but you must master it" (Gn 4:6-7). God did not appear to Adam and Eve as they wrestled with temptation, but he did appear to Cain, exhorting him not to go through with the contemplated act of violence.

But Cain does murder Abel, and God's response is swift and direct. Whereas the ground was cursed for Adam's sake, so that it would yield fruit only by the sweat of his brow, Cain is cursed from the ground—it would yield no fruit for him at all (Gn 4:11-12). Yet God protects even the life of the murderer

Cain, placing a mark on him "so that no one who found him would kill him" (Gn 4:15).

Despite God's judgment on Cain, human violence spreads. By the time of Noah, the earth is "full of violence" (Gn 6:11). Through the deluge, God meets man's unholy addiction to bloodshed with cataclysmic judgment. Humankind had profaned God's gift of life. Now God would deprive them of it. But in vowing never again to destroy all living creatures (Gn 8:21, 22), God placed himself squarely on the side of life.

Indeed, the scriptures underscore the value of human life in the account of Noah's departure from the ark. Having pronounced the Adamic blessings on Noah (Gn 9:1-3), God issues a command. "Whoever sheds the blood of man, by man shall his blood be shed; for in the image of God has God made man" (Gn 9:6). Human life may not be taken because it is made in God's image. This injunction is reiterated on Mt. Sinai. "Thou shalt not kill" (Ex 20:13), the sixth commandment teaches.

The premium placed on human life gives childbirth a redemptive dimension. Eve's seed will crush the serpent's head (Gn 3:15), Abraham's seed will inherit the promise (Gn 15:1-5), David's descendant will occupy Jerusalem's throne (2 Sm 7:12-16). The redemptive import of childbirth accounts for the many genealogies in scripture. Those genealogies chronicle the seed of the promise in faithful anticipation of the messianic age. It is fitting, therefore, that the New Testament commences with the "book of the genealogy of Jesus Christ," the promised seed (Mt 1:1).

The biblical affirmation that fertility is a blessing (Ex 23:26) and barrenness a curse (Gn 21:1ff) rests not on an agrarian or patriarchal ethic, but on the salvific hope of the ingathering of God's elect in Christ. Thus, Old Testament writers did not see biological reproduction as a mere natural event. Childbirth, for them, is a sign of God's favor. It is grace. And prenatal development is a season of divine activity.

For you created my inmost being;
   You knit me together in my mother's womb.
I praise you because I am fearfully and wonderfully made;
   your works are wonderful,
   I know that full well.
My frame was not hidden from you
   when I was made in the secret place.
When I was woven together in the depths of the earth,
   your eyes saw my unformed body. (Ps 139:13-16)

God's intimate involvement with the psalmist predated the psalmist's birth. God is at work during the period of gestation, fashioning another unique expression of his image. Other passages of scripture teach that God calls and equips people for service in his kingdom before they are born. God consecrated Jeremiah to a prophetic ministry while he was yet in his mother's womb (Jer 1:5). The Holy Spirit fills John the Baptist during Elizabeth's pregnancy (Lk 1:35, 39-45).

The scriptures also teach that Jesus was conceived by the Holy Spirit (Mt 1:20; Lk 1:35). For Jesus to become incarnate, to become truly human, he had to participate in the full range of human experience—from conception to death. Jesus' incarnation began at his conception. Thus, when Elizabeth, six months pregnant with John the Baptist, receives a visit from her cousin Mary, who is in the earliest stages of pregnancy with Jesus, she calls Mary "the mother of my Lord" (Lk 1:43).

The salvation Jesus brings—his words, his ministry, his very being—consists in life (Jn 14:6). To those who have drawn the wage of sin, whether in the form of death, disease, or privation, Jesus brings life: the life of the resurrection, which will at last swallow up death in victory (1 Cor 15:54). Reformed theologian John Murray has observed:

It is the sanctity of life that gives meaning to the redemptive process in all its phases. Life is forfeit by sin, and redemption is the redemption of forfeit life. God is not the God of the dead but of the living, and therefore those to whom he is God and who are his people must attain to the resurrection of the dead (Mk 12;27; Phil 3:11; Rom 8:17) . . . Forfeit life has been redeemed unto the securing and bestowal of life in the highest reaches of blessing and privilege conceivable for created beings.[43]

Belief in the sanctity of life is thus at the heart of the Christian tradition. Because of this, Christians of all theological persuasions in all ages have opposed abortion. Contemporary clergymen who advocate abortion on demand stand outside the stream of two millenia of Christian thought. "Those who conceal sexual wantonness by taking stimulating drugs to bring on an abortion," Clement of Alexandria, a second-century church father, wrote, "wholly lose their own humanity along with the fetus."[44] The second-century Epistle of Barnabas similarly forbids abortion. "Thou shalt not destroy thy conceptions before they are brought forth; nor kill them after they are born."[45] Athenagoras, another second-century father, cited the church's opposition to abortion as proof that the Lord's Supper, the eating and drinking of the body and blood of Jesus Christ, did not involve Christians in cannibalism.

How could we kill a man—we who say that women who take drugs to procure abortion are guilty of homicide and that they will have to answer to God for this abortion? One cannot at the same time believe that the fetus in the womb is a living being—as such in God's care— and kill one already brought forth into the light.[46]

The Reformers, too, opposed abortion. John Calvin wrote:

The fetus carried in the mother's womb is already a man; and it is quite unnatural that a life be destroyed of one who has not yet seen its enjoyment. For, it seems more unworthy that a man be killed in his home rather than in his field because for each man his home is his safest refuge. How much more abominable ought it to be considered to kill a fetus in the womb who has not yet been brought into the light?[47]

John Weemse, a seventeenth-century Protestant theologian, similarly taught, "It is a great cruelty to kill the child in the mother's belly."[48]

Twentieth-century churchmen have continued this tradition. "He who destroys germinating life kills a man," Karl Barth wrote in his *Church Dogmatics.*[49] Dietrich Bonhoeffer, who gave his life in opposition to the tyrannies of Nazism, said that social circumstances which can induce a woman to seek an abortion "cannot in any way alter the fact of murder."[50] Harvard Divinity School Professor George H. Williams summed up two millenia of Christian resistance to abortion when he wrote, "Two thousand years of Jewish-Christian history maintain that the fetus is a person with the right to life."

Abortion advocates are working to suppress that truth. Propagating the fiction that no one knows whether unborn children are human, they maintain that the unborn should have no legal protection. Abortion, they say, must be a private choice. The death of an unborn child should concern no one save the abortionist and the woman who contracts for his or her services. What they are really saying, as we have seen, is that some human lives are not worth protecting.

Christians cannot abide that view. We cannot ignore the shedding of innocent blood because God does not ignore it. God has taken sides—the side of the oppressed (Ps 10:17, 18), of the weak (Ps 82:4), of the fatherless (Ps 82:3). "Whatsoever you do to the least of these, my brethren," Jesus says, "you have done to me" (Mt 25:40). Jesus' identification with those for whom society has no regard constrains us to take up the cause of the unborn. Resistance to abortion is no mere option for the Christian. It is an imperative.

SIX

Rationalizing Infanticide: Medical Ethics in the Eighties

James Manney

It's the same old business of the runt of the litter getting pushed away from the teat. —*James T. Burtchaell*

THE FACT OF INFANTICIDE burst on the public consciousness in dramatic fashion in April, 1982, when a mentally impaired infant was allowed to starve to death in Bloomington Hospital in Indiana. The parents of "Infant Doe," believing that Down's Syndrome children never have a minimally acceptable quality of life, refused to authorize routine surgery that would have allowed their son to eat normally. They further directed that their son not be fed intravenously. Two courts, including the Indiana State Supreme Court, sanctioned this "nontreatment," and Bloomington Hospital allowed the parents' orders to be carried out. Infant Doe died of starvation six days after birth.[1]

The Infant Doe infanticide is not unique. In 1976, Dr. C. Everett Koop, then a noted Philadelphia pediatric surgeon and now the U.S. Surgeon General, told members of the American Academy of Pediatrics, which had given him an award, that "you all know that infanticide is being practiced right *now* in this country." In the years since, numerous other cases of infanticide or attempted infanticide became public.[2]

Indeed a new pro-infanticide ethic seems to be taking hold in the medical profession. The medical literature of the 1970s held many shocks for those who thought that a physician always went to bat for babies in tough spots.

—In 1973, Dr. Raymond Duff and Dr. A.G.M. Campbell reported that fourteen percent of the infant deaths in their intensive care nursery at Yale-New Haven Hospital were caused by deliberate withholding or withdrawal of treatment. In some cases this meant denial of food and water—starvation. The pediatricians thought this was wise policy.[3]

—A majority of pediatricians and pediatric surgeons answering a survey said they would not treat a baby like Infant Doe if the parents wanted him to die.[4]

—Half the pediatricians answering surveys in Massachusetts and in the San Francisco Bay area would not operate on a Down's Syndrome baby with an intestinal obstruction. A third thought they should be allowed to kill such infants directly.[5]

—It was reported that most spina bifida babies in Great Britain and many in the U.S. do not receive corrective and life-saving surgery because physicians and parents thought their quality of life will be too low.[6]

—In 1974, 17 of 20 medical people and bioethicists meeting in Sonoma Valley, California, said they would support direct killing of infants in some circumstances. Only one member of this elite group flatly opposed direct killing.[7]

Further evidence that physicians were sympathetic to a new ethic came in the wake of the Infant Doe case. The federal government opened a 24-hour toll-free phone to receive reports of suspected infanticide and issued rules requiring hospitals to post warnings that discriminatory nontreatment of handicapped infants was forbidden. The American Academy of Pediatrics loudly protested these "Baby Doe rules" and successfully sued in federal court to block them. When the government invited comments on revised rules, 72 percent of the pediatricians who commented opposed them.[8]

Infanticide has been seen as a journalistic sensation, a courtroom drama, a power struggle between physicians and the government, a new civil rights issue, a cause celebre in the prolife movement, a new issue for disability rights advocates, and something of a scandal for many physicians. Less attention has been paid to the ethics of infanticide, particularly the role certain philosophers and theologians have played in formulating the new medical ethic.

The truth is that infanticide has become a widespread problem largely because ethicists have provided a rationale for eliminating defective infants. Doctors look to specialists in bioethics for guidance in the treatment of handicapped newborns. So do parents. So do policy-makers and hospital administrators. Acts that would otherwise be unthinkable become thinkable when moralists say they are justified.

Ethicists also articulate "new" values. Indeed, this is one of the most important reasons why we should pay attention to them and understand what they are saying. The ethics of infanticide in particular has become a frontier where new ideas about human life and human community are being explored and tried out. Ethical issues press urgently in the nursery. What claim do the helpless have on us? What is valuable about human life? What *is* human life? Liberated from Judeo-Christian moral foundations, some ethicists are offering new answers to these old questions—answers which will affect all of us.

There is no doubt that some bioethicists hold highly disturbing views about the moral worth of handicapped infants. The following is a sampling of what "the best and the brightest" are saying to rationalize the intentional taking of innocent newborn life:

Bioethicist Peter Singer, writing in the prestigious medical journal *Pediatrics*: "If we compare a severely defective human infant with a nonhuman animal, a dog or pig, for example, we will often find the nonhuman to have superior capacities, both actual and potential, for rationality, self-consciousness, and anything else that can plausibly be considered morally significant."[9]

Glanville Williams, jurist and moralist at Cambridge University: "An eugenic killing by a mother, exactly parallelled by the bitch that kills her mis-shapen puppies, cannot confidently be pronounced immoral."[10]

Michael Tooley, professor of philosophy at Stanford University: "The practical moral problem can ... be satisfactorily handled by choosing some period of time, such as a week after birth, as the interval during which infanticide will be permitted."[11]

Tristram Englehardt, philosopher and physician at the Kennedy Institute, Georgetown University: "[The decision about treatment] belongs properly to the parents because the child belongs to them in a sense that it does not belong to anyone else, even to itself. ... Clinical and parental judgment may and should be guided by the expected lifestyle and the cost (in parental and societal pain and money) of its attainment."[12]

Author Marvin Kohl: "Beneficent euthanasia is a prima facie obligation. This means that in certain circumstances we have an actual moral obligation to induce death."[13]

It is tempting to dismiss such opinions as grotesque musings by eccentric academics. This would be a mistake, for they are voicing a new ethic that has come to dominate ethical thinking in the medical profession.

The "new medical ethic" was described in the journal *California Medicine* in 1970.[14] The anonymous editorialist thought that the medical profession was caught between two ethics. The old ethic, nurtured by the Judeo-Christian moral tradition, "placed great emphasis on the intrinsic worth and equal value of every human life regardless of its stage or condition." This traditional view is commonly referred to as the "sanctity of life ethic." Opposing it is a "quality of life" ethic that would make it "necessary and acceptable to place relative rather than absolute values on such things as human lives."

What defines a particular individual's "quality of life?" The writer anticipated that the definition would involve judgments about the individual's capacity for personal fulfillment, the common welfare, the preservation of the environment, and the betterment of the species.

This writer was prophetic. Babies have in fact been killed for all the reasons he cited: because others think a handicapped infant's life is not worth living, because the burdens of raising handicapped children will interfere with the personal well-being of their parents and siblings, and because disabled people are unproductive and expensive social burdens.

Bioethicists give other reasons as well. Some simply do not think that impaired babies are human persons.

Professor Michael Tooley thinks it unfortunate that most people use the terms "person" and "human being" interchangeably. *Persons* have rights (including a right to life), according to Tooley, but not every *human being* can properly be regarded as a *person*. To tell the difference, Tooley lays down a rule: "An organism possesses a serious right to life only if it possesses the concept of a self as a continuing subject of experiences and other mental states, and believes that it is itself such a continuing entity." On this basis, Tooley, would allow infanticide up to a week after birth.

While Tooley disposes of human infants, he worries about animals. Since animals can be self-conscious and conceive of themselves as continuing entities, they may possess a right to life not accorded to a human infant. Tooley warns: "One may find himself driven to conclude that our everyday treatment of animals is morally indefensible, and that we are in fact murdering innocent persons."[15]

If Tooley doubts the personhood of the handicapped baby, Joseph Fletcher doubts even the child's humanity. Fletcher provides the confused modernist with no less than fifteen criteria to make the critical judgment about whether someone is human. Among them: minimal intelligence, a sense of the future, a sense of the past, a capacity to relate to others, concern for others, and a balance between rationality and feeling. He is vague about what some of these criteria mean, but is specific about others. For example, a human being with an I.Q. of 40 is only questionably a person; below the 20 mark, he is definitely *not* a person.[16]

Some ethicists who write about these issues are not much concerned about handicapped infants at all. They are apologists for mercy-killing. Disabled newborns are one of several classes of people who they think deserve a speedy and painless death. Their task is to make the naturally repellant idea of killing the helpless a reasonable, even admirable, "option"— much like the eugenic killing of miscellaneous undesirables in Nazi Germany preceded the wholesale attack on the Jewish race.

Tristram Englehardt, an ethicist who is both a philosopher and a physician, argues that society must find a way to put handicapped children to death. Englehardt makes the astounding argument that killing is an ethical imperative *from the child's point of view*. A handicapped child, he writes, "has a right not to have its life prolonged."[17]

Others echo Englehardt. "Why should the no-code designation be preferred over the injection?" asks philosopher James Rachels.[18] Some moralists hold that we are sometimes morally compelled to kill. "Beneficent euthanasia is a prima facie obligation," argues Marvin Kohl.[19]

These ideas are not confined to scrupulously secular sources. Daniel Maguire, a Catholic theologian teaching at a Catholic university, maintains that it may be moral and should be legal to accelerate the death process by injecting poison or overdosing patients with morphine.[20] (Maguire, of course, does not represent Catholic teaching on this matter.)

Behind these confused statements lies an unabashed utilitarianism, the view that objective moral norms are irrelevant in determining right and wrong. Rather, the utilitarian believes that the righteous act is the one which brings the greatest good to the greatest number of people.

Professor Fletcher, for example, offers the following as his guiding principle: "Human happiness and well-being is the highest good or *summum bonum*, and . . . therefore any ends or purposes which that ideal or standard validates are just, right, good." Suicide and mercy killing are acceptable in this scheme, as is infanticide. Such acts are not regrettable necessities or grimy compromises with one's conscience, but positive human goods. "It comes down to this," Fletcher writes, "that in some situations a morally good end can justify a relatively 'bad' means."[21]

Many bioethicists today think this way. To speak to them of "rights" and "equality" is to speak a different language.

But the greatest difference is in world view. The boldest of these bioethicists articulate a new vision of human life which contrasts starkly with the Judeo-Christian value system, which has nourished the West for two thousand years. The first step, says Joseph Fletcher, is to rid ourselves of that obsolete view "according to which God is not only the cause but also the builder of nature and its works, and not only the builder but even the manager."

Once they are rid of God, ethicists are free to make up new moral rules. Marvin Kohl, for example, thinks mercy-killing advances human dignity, if dignity is understood in Kohl's special sense as something synonomous with one's ability to control his own life. In order to assert his dignity, a man might want to kill himself, or have himself killed if he is comatose or bedridden because then he is no longer in control. We can kill such a person mercifully, says Kohl, in respect for his "dignity."[22]

Tristram Englehardt believes that we have moral duties not to give existence to other persons (and to take existence from them) precisely because it is in our power to do so. "Humans can now control reproduction," he writes. "One must now decide when and under what circumstances persons will come into existence." For Englehardt, deciding whether to let a handicapped newborn live is simply one aspect of birth control.[23]

Joseph Fletcher describes the clash of value systems, or world views, most starkly. On the one hand is a "simplistic" view which holds that "living and dying are in God's hands and that life is God's to give and only God's to take." On the other is "humanistic medicine," with its ethic of responsibility, including "responsibility for the termination of subhuman life in posthuman beings."[24]

Fletcher believes that infanticide is acceptable because human beings have a moral obligation to increase human well-being wherever possible. Questions of human rights should not interfere. "All rights are imperfect and can be set aside if human need requires it," he says in one of his essays on human life. Fletcher thinks that man's mastery of technology makes him truly human. "A baby made artificially," he remarks, "by deliberate and careful contrivance, would be more *human* than one resulting from sexual roulette."[25]

Fletcher and bioethicists like him have at least one point to commend them: they confess their creed straightforwardly and unabashedly. When they describe handicapped infants as subhuman organisms devoid of rights, there is no mistaking their meaning. Theirs is an ethic of human will and power. "It's the same old business of the runt of the litter getting pushed away from the teat," says theologian James Burtchaell.[26]

Other ethicists who have addressed the issue of the treatment of disabled newborns are more subtle than Fletcher and Tooley and less willing to jettison the Judeo-Christian ethical tradition. Because they are perceived to operate more or less within traditional ethics, these thinkers have exercised great influence over medical thinking about bioethical questions. Yet the answers they offer are much the same, and their work is even more corrosive than that of the unrestrained radicals precisely because their influence is so great.

Indeed, the authority of professional ethicists stands out in a guideline about the treatment of handicapped newborns issued by the American Medical Association in 1981. The guideline, entitled "Quality of Life," gave this advice to pediatricians confronted with a baby with physical or mental impairments:

> In caring for defective infants, the advice and judgment of the physician should be readily available but the decision whether to treat a severely defective infant and exert maximal efforts to sustain life should be the choice of the parents. The parents should be told the options, expected benefits, risks, and limits of any proposed care, *how the potential for human relationships is affected by the infant's condition* and relevant information and answers to their questions.[27] (Emphasis added.)

The phrase "how the potential for human relationships is affected by the infant's condition" has become known as the "relational principle." It is a vague phrase, open to endless subjective interpretations, quite out of place in a medical statement. The relational principle does not, in fact, come from a medical source at all. It was formulated by the most influential of the bioethicists who have addressed the problem of handicapped newborns—a Jesuit priest named Richard McCormick.

Unlike the ethicists we have already heard from, Fr. McCormick reasons lucidly and carefully, makes no outrageous statements, and mounts no quixotic assault on traditional ethics. Indeed, he starts from the most traditional ethical authority of all—the Christian scriptures. As a Christian he believes that men were created to serve higher purposes: to love God and to love their neighbor—two loves that are inseparable. He quotes 1 John 4:20-21: "If any man says I love God and hates his brother, he is a liar. For he who loves not his brother, whom he sees, how can he love God whom he does not see?"

From this, Fr. McCormick draws some striking conclusions.

"It is in others that God demands to be recognized and loved," he says. "If this is true, it means that, in Judeo-Christian perspective, the meaning, substance and consummation of life is found in human *relationships*, and the qualities of justice, respect, concern, compassion, and support that surround them."[28]

Writing in the *Journal of the American Medical Association*, Fr. McCormick lays down a relational principle for handicapped newborns.

A life that is "painful, poverty-stricken and deprived, away from home and friends, oppressive," might well be a life of which it could be said that "human relationships—which are the very possibility of growth in love of God and neighbor—would be so threatened, strained or submerged that they would no longer function as the heart and meaning of the individual's life as they should." In such cases, the Christian can say that life has achieved its potential, and the individual can be allowed to die. This guideline, he hopes, "may help in decisions about sustaining the lives of grossly deformed and deprived infants."

Grossly deformed and deprived? What does that mean? How indeed can healthy adults with no experience of disability imagine the quality and value of relationships a handicapped baby might have in future years?

Fr. McCormick is not insensitive to the difficulty of answering such questions, but he unhelpfully places the burden of proof on the infant. He approves a surgeon's opinion that "if a severely handicapped child were suddenly given one moment of omniscience and total awareness of his or her outlook for the future, would that child necessarily opt for life? No one has yet been able to demonstrate that the answer would always be 'yes.'"

Of course no one can demonstrate that; it is an entirely speculative question, and Fr. McCormick may well be right to say that some infants would choose to die "in some instances."[29] The question is: in what instances? There is another question: would it make any moral difference if Fr. McCormick or anyone else could identify such infants? The prospect of a medical ethic that permits killing people because they do not want to live is hardly appealing.

The fact is that the relational principle is deficient in practice as well as in theory. People will always draw the line about relationships in different places. For example, what about an Infant Doe: a baby with an irreparable chromosomal disorder, a correctable but life-threatening complication, and parents who are convinced that the child's relational capacity will be substandard? How can the relational principle insist that he have surgery if the operation will do nothing to improve his capacity for relationships?

Whether these relationships will be substandard is simply a matter of opinion. Fr. McCormick would demand the operation. He was harsh on the authorities responsible for the Infant Doe case, calling it "nothing less than a state-authored deprivation of innocent life without either due process of law or the equal protection of the laws."[30] As infanticide has become more common, he has issued many cautions: Babies should not die because their families cannot cope with them; retarded babies should not be left to starve because they are retarded; nontreatment decisions are not private matters as doctors claim; the courts can properly intervene when decision-makers behave irresponsibly.[31]

But nothing in the relational principle compels anyone to agree with Fr. McCormick about any of this.

As Dennis Horan, a lawyer and co-editor of *Death, Dying, and Euthanasia,* points out, "there is no way that this relational principle can be less than a death warrant for some retardates except in the hands of Fr. McCormick himself."[32] But the problem is deeper than that. The relational principle is no principle at all. It falls apart as soon as one begins to apply it to specific cases.

It is worth trying to understand how Fr. McCormick went wrong in his ethical reasoning. One of his mistakes was to focus too narrowly on so-called hard cases—those rare situations where the infant's disabilities are truly severe and the medical prognosis genuinely perplexing. We often think about hard cases when we consider these problems, and doctors who want to ease handicapped babies into death often emphasize the plight of those who are in the worst condition.

Lawyers have a wise saying: "hard cases make bad law." They mean that laws made to deal with bizarre, unusual, or extreme cases are often irrelevant or even unjust when applied to more common situations. Ethicists who lay down rules for letting handicapped newborns die should heed this aphorism.

Fr. McCormick concentrates on hard cases in the intensive care nursery and he describes them in highly emotive language. They are infants whose lives can be sustained, "but in a wretched, painful, or deformed condition," babies who might have "a terribly mutilated body from birth" or face "a life that is from birth one long, painful, oppressive convalescence."[33]

Who are these babies? Fr. McCormick describes them in these infinitely tragic terms:

> In neonatal intensive care units . . . we are dealing with tiny patients who have no history, have had no chance at life, and have no say in the momentous decision about their treatment. Some are born with anomalies or birth accidents so utterly devastating (especially extensive brain damage) that they will never rise much above the "persistent vegetative state."[34]

It is seriously misleading to suggest that babies like these are the typical patients in neonatal intensive care units. These "tiny patients" do exist—at least for a brief period—and deciding whether and how to treat them can be genuinely difficult. There can be some superficial plausibility in considering the capacity for relationships of an infant so badly damaged that it will not be able to interact with the world in any way. Yet a relational principle formulated for them should not be applied to most of the handicapped infants born in the U.S. each day.

Fr. McCormick and other bioethicists who would introduce "quality of life" considerations into neonatal treatment decisions make other unsound assumptions as well. Two key themes run through their thinking. One is opposition to what they call "vitalism." Joseph Fletcher defines vitalism as the proposition that "we are always obliged to prolong life as much as possible."[35] The second theme is great distress over the effect of medical technology. The ethical dilemmas in the nursery, these ethicists say, are caused by the new ability of physicians to rescue babies who would have died in years past.

Both notions deserve the most careful scrutiny.

Fr. John J. Paris, a theologian and sometime collaborator with Fr. McCormick, rejects vitalism on religious grounds. It is idolatry, he says, to view death as an unmitigated evil and life as an absolute good. Vitalism makes life "an end and a goal in itself, a new golden calf before which we may worship."[36]

Advanced medical technology, moreover, has given vitalists dangerous tools, he says. Seriously handicapped and diseased babies died swiftly in years past because nothing could be done for them. Things are different now. We face entirely new ethical problems. Fr. Paris says that the ethical task is to stop modern doctors from using technological tools to preserve every life they possibly can, regardless of the patient's prospects. "When the difficult questions concerning the appropriate care of defective neonates arise," he says, "the easiest solution is simply to do everything technology allows: plug the kid in. That way, one is absolved from having to make difficult decisions."[37]

Fr. Paris advances the remarkable proposition that the

prolife movement is to blame for these problems. Prolifers, he argues, have successfully pressured medical people into agreeing "that life is ultimate and that everything possible must be done to sustain it." The result? Prolifers "are responsible for creating disastrous coma ward situations in this country which will soon become so abhorrent that there will be a public outcry to stop the madness by actively terminating the lives of such victims of our technology."

What is to be done? Fr. McCormick and Fr. Paris would establish broad guidelines to allow physicians and parents to make "quality of life" judgments about handicapped infants.[38]

But is this an accurate picture of the problem in the intensive care nursery?

A rigid insistence that biological life must be prolonged at all costs has never been a part of good medical care. Doctors and nurses deal with dying patients all the time. They continually make *medical* judgments about whether therapies will be useful. When further treatment is pointless, doctors will usually cease life-sustaining efforts and allow a patient to die peacefully. As ethicist Paul Ramsey says, those caring for the dying "need only to be sensitive and apt to determine when attempts to cure or save life are no longer indicated—that is, when in place of any longer bothering the dying with vain treatments, the indicated medical care calls upon us to surround them instead with a human presence while they die."[39]

It would be hard to find a good physician who would disagree with that statement and conduct his care of the dying in any other way. Of course, it can be difficult to decide when someone is in the process of dying. Family members can insist that doctors "do everything" when the right medical decision may be to let the individual die. But few doctors favor this approach. To the contrary, most deplore it. There is certainly no evidence that the problem is so serious that we must replace medical judgments with subjective "quality of life" guidelines to decide when people should die.

Indeed, it is not a commitment to vitalism that leads those

who affirm the sanctity of human life to object to the killing or nontreatment of handicapped newborns. The babies who are targets for infanticide are not dying. Their lives are threatened for *social reasons*—not because of their medical condition.

What about technology, Fr. Paris's "disasterous coma ward situations" where doctors automatically "plug the kid in?"

Technology is also a largely irrelevant issue in infanticide for the same reasons that the charge of "vitalism" misses the point. Desperate and mistaken attempts to save life at all costs are *not* problems in nurseries where parents and physicians skeptically assess the quality of life of certain newborn infants. Infant Doe and other victims that we know about died because medical technology that would have been applied to "normal" babies was *not* made available to them.

But concern about medical technology is not completely beside the point here. In fact, we are concerned about infanticide in large part because new medical technology allows physicians to rescue many *more* seriously ill newborns today than they could twenty years ago. Almost all spina bifida infants would have died before 1960. Today almost all can be saved. Very tiny premature infants who would invariably have died in the past can now be sustained in modern neonatal intensive care units.

But are the ethical issues involved in the decision of *whether* to use such technology really different than they have always been? A physician today ponders whether to recommend a low-risk but recently-perfected operation to close the hole in a spina bifida child's spine. Forty years ago he might have wondered whether it was worth using newly-developed antibiotics to treat the same child's meningitis. In both cases, he may face the temptation to let the child die for "quality of life" reasons—for some reason other than a medical indication. As one professor of pediatrics comments, "neonatology has always had its ethical problems."[40]

It is doubtful whether medical technology has created *new* ethical problems in the intensive care nursery, though it may have created *more* of them. Technology forces physicians to ask the ethical questions more frequently and insistently. The questions still need to be answered. The increasing popularity of "nontreatment" is caused by an erosion in ethics, not by an escalation in technology.

Fr. McCormick, Fr. Paris, and other bioethicists claim that the guidance they offer about the treatment of handicapped newborns draws on the classic moral distinction between "ordinary" and "extraordinary" means of treatment. This concept was developed by Catholic theologians to help people judge when medical treatment imposed excessive burdens and could therefore be withheld or refused.

Thus, the argument goes, life-saving treatment of handicapped newborns is often "extraordinary" and therefore not morally required. Some who make this argument do not claim to speak from an avowedly Christian viewpoint, but rather adopt this religiously-grounded idea in order to lend a higher moral authority to what is really a radically utilitarian view. Others do seek to make a specifically Christian ethical statement which is used for pastoral counseling, among other purposes. It is a curious fact, for example, that many of the parents involved in such cases have been Catholics, and they often claim church sanction for their decisions to let their handicapped babies die.[41]

The distinction between ordinary and extraordinary means is a common sensical idea: no one is morally obliged to use all conceivable treatments to preserve his life, but only those treatments that offer a reasonable hope of success and do not impose excessive burdens. A person with a brain tumor is not obliged to have an operation that might save his life but leave him with severe mental impairment. A terminally ill heart patient can morally choose to die rather than undergo experimental heart surgery. On the other hand, a blood transfusion for an accident victim or an operation that has a good chance of excising a malignant tumor are usually classified as ordinary treatment. Patients should submit to them out of respect for their own lives (and often for the sake of loved ones). Those who make medical decisions on others' behalf—parents of minor children, for example—are under the same obligation.

It is clearly an abuse of the ordinary/extraordinary principle to claim, as some ethicists have, that an operation which carries few risks suddenly becomes an excessively burdensome medical procedure when proposed for a handicapped infant. "Burdensome" in this branch of moral philosophy refers to the anticipated impact of the treatment *on the patient.* The infanticide ethicists would twist this to mean that the *success* of surgery would be burdensome *to the families* because it preserves the life of an infant the parents do not want.

Some ethicists argue that such treatment is excessively burdensome because it inflicts a burdensome life on the child. But this suggests that life with physical and mental impairments is an inferior life. Such a belief is rooted in prejudice against handicapped people.

Some ethicists also argue that operations like those denied Infant Doe are "extraordinary" because the patient will still be handicapped even after a successful operation. But "reasonable benefit" refers to the probability that the medical treatment will accomplish its purpose. It may not solve all the patient's medical problems, but it is not ethically extraordinary if it will solve some of them for a patient who is not dying.[42]

The truth is that the distinction between ordinary and extraordinary means is primarily intended to answer difficult medical questions at the end of life—not the beginning. It is for the gravely ill or critically injured patient who must weigh the burdens and benefits of a proposed treatment that may not cure him, may well hurt him, and would burden his family besides. A serious medical condition—cancer, heart disease, an accident—has made his condition terminal. The treatment is "extraordinary" because it won't do much for him.

The situation is almost exactly reversed for the handicapped newborn. The treatment is called "extraordinary" because it *will* help. It is the decision not to treat that makes his condition terminal. A non-medical factor—his projected I.Q., a doctor's or philosopher's ideas about meaningful life, his parents' aspirations—make him unwanted. Social reasons, not medical indications, make his treatment "extraordinary."

The issue, in other words, is not whether dying infants should have high-risk, painful operations. No one is arguing that such operations should be performed routinely. Rather, the ethical issue is whether handicapped infants should receive the same treatment non-handicapped infants receive. The corresponding theological issue is whether we are going to allow a quality of life ethic to replace the traditional sanctity of life ethic.

Such is the noxious moral climate in which infanticide has flourished. The current struggle is between conflicting ideas about what it means to be human and what it takes to live in human community. The ethicists who would rationalize infanticide are elitists. To be "human" in their definition would require men and women to be more than merely human. Although they shroud their intentions in euphemisms and frame their criteria for death in elusively subjective terms, their ethics are really anti-ethics. They attack the foundations of human life and community. And their materialistic, utilitarian, radically secular vision is now aggressively ascendent.

The truth is that a disabled baby struggling for life is a human being. Most of us, despite the efforts of situation ethicists and radical utilitarians, are still able to recognize this otherwise obvious fact. Despite sickness or handicaps or probable social circumstances in later life, the disabled child is one of us, a creature of God, a pearl of great price.

Here indeed we have one of "the least of these" to whom the Galilean so profoundly referred almost two thousand years ago. It is imperative that men and women of good will affirm this truth and rise to their defense.

SEVEN

Ideological Biases in Today's Theories of Moral Education

Paul Vitz

T HIS CHAPTER PRESENTS a critical evaluation of the two most influential theories of moral education operating in the United States today. The first theory is commonly known as Values Clarification (VC); the second is the model of moral development proposed by Lawrence Kohlberg. Both of these theories have been developed in the last twenty years or so by secular thinkers, and have generally been assumed to be neutral, scientific, and otherwise unbiased. That this is far from the truth has been made clear in recent scholarly and popular writing,[1] and is the theme of this chapter.

Values Clarification

General Background

This approach to moral education is due primarily to the efforts of Louis E. Raths and Sidney B. Simon, in collaboration with several colleagues.[2] All the developers of Values Clarification are professors of education or on the staff of institutes of education.[3] First developed in the 1960s, VC's widespread use in the public school system did not come until the mid and late 1970s. Its authors point out their position had its origin in "the thinking of John Dewey."[4] Very generally, VC is a set of related procedures

> . . . designed to engage students and teachers in the active formulation and examination of values. It does not teach a particular set of values. There is no sermonizing or moralizing. The goal is to involve students in practical experiences, making them aware of *their own* feelings, *their own* ideas, *their own* beliefs, so that the choices and decisions they make are conscious and deliberate, based on *their own* value systems.[5]

As this passage demonstrates, Values Clarification is contrasted with the direct teaching of morals or ethics (sermonizing) which Simon and Raths reject as a hopelessly outdated form of "inculcation of the adults' values upon the young [*sic*]."[6] This position is outdated, they say, because today's complex society presents so many inconsistent sources of values. Thus, it is argued, "parents offer one set of shoulds and should nots. The church often suggests another. The peer group offers a third view of values. Hollywood and the popular magazines, a fourth . . . The spokesmen for the new Left and the counterculture, an eighth; and on and on."[7]

In the context of this confusing contemporary scene the developers of VC reject moralizing; they also reject indifference to the problem of values, since a *laissez-faire* position just ignores the problem and leaves students vulnerable to unexamined influences from the popular culture. Instead, it is argued that what students need is a process which will enable them to select the best and reject the worst in terms of their own values and special circumstances.[8]

In order to enable young people to "build their own value system," Raths's system focuses on the "valuing process."[9] Valuing, according to these theorists, is composed of three basic processes which are briefly summarized as follows:

PRIZING one's beliefs and behaviors
   1. prizing and cherishing
   2. publicly affirming, when appropriate
CHOOSING one's beliefs and behaviors
   3. choosing from alternatives
   4. choosing after consideration of consequences
   5. choosing freely
ACTING on one's beliefs
   6. acting
   7. acting with a pattern, consistency, and repetition[10]

At the essence of the VC approach to moral education is its claim to "values neutrality." Rather than instilling particular values, the stated goal is to allow students to understand and affirm whatever their individual beliefs and values might be. In order to accomplish this, the VC theorists propose a series of exercises, called "strategies," which represent the major contribution of their recent writings.[11]

Psychological and Philosophical Assumptions

First, it is significant that the processes proposed by the VC theorists are in this order: prizing, choosing, and acting. That is, there is little, if any, attention given to what the students' initial values are or where they came from; rather, the first emphasis is on prizing already existing values. The theorists use the term "pride" as a synonym for prizing;[12] there is almost no attention given to whether the student's values are *worth* prizing. (That would obviously raise the *bete noire* of absolute values.) Neither do the second and third processes (choosing and acting) constitute an adequate basis for evaluation of or reflection upon what even VC proponents assume are the student's initially confused values. This is particularly true since the main thrust of Values Clarification is on consequences for the 'autonomous self.' As a result, like all form of moral relativism, this process does not encourage serious rational reflection. Instead, it begins with the irrational, emotional prizing of whatever the student already happens to have as values or goals; and the secondary purpose of evaluation of consequences is overshadowed by the initial prizing and by the emphasis on self-acceptance.

Although the psychological and, one should add, educational assumptions of the VC theorists are rarely presented and to my knowledge have never been explicitly defended, they are nevertheless essential to this approach to moral education. At the center of Values Clarification, as at the center of most relativistic value systems, is a particular concept of *the self,* with a strong emphasis on self-expression and self-realization. The way in which this relates to educational theory has been the subject of study by the Christian philosopher Nicholas Wolterstorff:

> ... The fundamental position is that each self comes with various innate desires and interests, that mental health and happiness will be achieved if these desires are allowed to find their satisfaction within the natural and social environment, and that an individual's mental health and happiness constitute the ultimate good for him. . . . What must at all costs be avoided ... is the imposition on someone of the rules and expectations of other people. That way lies unhappiness and disease. The road to that ultimate good which is personal health and happiness is the road of self-expression, not the road of internalization of others' rules.
> ... The proper goal of the educator, then, is to provide the child with an environment which is *permissive,* in that there is no attempt to impose the rules of others onto the child, and which is *nourishing* in that the environment provides for

the satisfaction of the child's desires and interests.

. . . According to some, a permissive and nourishing school environment is all the child needs. For others, however, persons characteristically develop internal blockages or inhibitions of their natural desires and interests, thereby leading to mental disease and unhappiness; and the school should work to remove inhibitions to self-expression in addition to providing a permissive nourishing environment.[13]

Advocates of Values Clarification hold this latter view (that inhibitions ought to be actively challenged and removed to insure personal health and wholeness). Thus, the VC "strategies" are designed to question, and to lead to the rejection of, any inhibiting beliefs or values which the student might have picked up from home, church, or elsewhere. If parents object to the undermining of religious and moral training in the VC exercises, well then, parents must be in favor of psychological neurosis, moral indoctrination, and educational backwardness. Therefore, not surprisingly, parents are often regarded as a major part of the problem in this vision for the progressive enlightenment of the nation's children.

The view that the self is intrinsically good, that corruption comes only from an imperfect environment or circumstances, is traceable at least to Rousseau, and was cultivated and spread through the nineteenth century, particularly in the thought of the Romantics. Today this sanguine view of human nature dominates much of American psychotherapy, popular psychology, and educational theory. From Rogerian therapy to Gestalt therapy to Transactional Analysis to EST (Erhard Seminar Training) to open classrooms and values clarification, "selfist" therapists and educators have sought to promote mental health and happiness through the magic door of "self-expression."[14] Remove inhibitions, tolerate moral pluralism, let each do his own thing, and all will be well.

In spite of its popularity, however, it is noteworthy that

most serious psychologists have been consistently critical of such humanistic self-theory, and recent criticisms have been particularly strong.[15] The central thrust of these critiques has been twofold. First, there is substantial objective evidence that man is *not* intrinsically entirely good. Instead, human nature appears to include a significant natural component of selfishness, narcissism, aggressiveness, etc. Evidence for this is widely accepted by psychoanalysts and psychiatrists of many different persuasions, whether or not they ground their views in religious doctrine such as a belief in "original sin" (as most, indeed, do not). The clinical evidence assembled over many years from a large and heterogeneous group of people for such behaviors as sadism, destructiveness, and violent fantasies and dreams is simply too great to sustain such a naive view of human nature. Instead of convoluted explanations about how environment or circumstances cause antisocial behavior, it is more economical from a theoretical point of view simply to accept the intrinsic dual nature of man, a view which is, incidentally, consistent with orthodox Jewish and Christian teaching on the subject.

An additional weakness is that the unabashed ethical relativism of the Values Clarification approach to moral education ultimately contradicts itself in certain basic respects. The most obvious contradiction is that in spite of the alleged relativity of all values, the theorists clearly believe that their approach has unique value; that is, that students *should* engage in their VC program, they *should* prize their program of how to clarify values, etc. Raths et al. attack values-pushing by teachers and yet they urge teachers to push the value of clarifying values by using their system. Indeed, when they argue for their system they are being moralizing and sermonizing like anyone else. They criticize values inculcation as "selling," "forcing one's pet values" on children at the price of free inquiry, reason, etc.[16] But when it comes to the value of *their* position, the implications of the relativity of all values including their own is not addressed. (That is, they overlook the absurdity of saying, "There are no absolute values." Their own statement contradicts itself.)

Another basic contradiction in the Values Clarification system also derives from its relativist and anti-value assumptions. The VC systems penchant for subjectivism ends up— oddly, but perhaps predictably enough—in authoritarianism,[17] even, or even especially, between parents and children. As Raths has written:

> . . . If a child says that he likes something, *it does not seem appropriate* for an older person to say, 'You shouldn't like that.' Or, if a child should say, 'I am interested in that,' *it does not seem quite right* for an older person to say to him, 'You shouldn't be interested in things like that.'
>
> . . . As a matter of fact, in a society like ours, governed by our Constitution, teachers *might well see themselves as obliged to support the idea* that every *individual is entitled* to the views that he has and to the values that he holds, especially where these have been examined and affirmed. Is this not the cornerstone of what we mean by a free society? . . . We say be authoritative in those areas that deal with truth and falsity. In areas involving aspirations, purposes, attitudes, interests, beliefs, etc., we may raise questions, but *we cannot* 'lay down the law' about what a child's values should be. By definition and *by social right,* then, values are personal things.[18] (Note all the moralizing in the underlined words.)

However, when Raths et al. bring up the question of whether the child should be allowed to choose anything he wishes, they answer in the negative. Parents and teachers do have. the right [sic] to set some "choices" as off-limits, according to the values clarifiers. But they don't have this right because the child's choices are wrong. Instead, they say that they have this right because certain choices could be *intolerable* to the parent or teacher. As Wolterstorff cogently concludes, thus does their position "turn into arbitrary authority."[19] The only rationale for the forbidding of a particular choice is that the teacher or parent finds the choice personally offensive or inconvenient, as illustrated in the following example from the VC literature:

Teacher: So some of you think it is best to be honest on tests, is that right? (Some heads nod affirmatively.) And some of you think dishonesty is all right? (A few hesitant and slight nods.) And I guess some of you are not certain. (Heads nod.) . . .

Ginger: Does that mean that we can decide for ourselves whether we should be honest on tests here?

Teacher: No, that means that you can decide on the value. I personally value honesty; and although you may choose to be dishonest, I shall insist that we be honest on our tests here. In other areas of your life, you may have more freedom to be dishonest, but one can't do anything any time, and in this class I shall expect honesty on tests.

Ginger: But then how can we decide for ourselves? Aren't you telling us what to value?

Sam: Sure, you're telling us what we should do and believe in.

Teacher: Not exactly, I don't mean to tell you what you should value. That's up to you. But I do mean that in this class, not elsewhere necessarily, you have to be honest on tests or suffer certain consequences. I merely mean that I cannot give tests without the rule of honesty. All of you who choose dishonesty as a value may not practice it here, that's all I'm saying. Further questions anyone?[20]

From this flabbergasting example, we might suggest as analogies, "You may or may not steal in other stores, but I shall expect and insist on honesty in my store." Likewise, "You are not to be a racist or you are not to hate Jews in my class, but elsewhere—that is up to you." You may have more freedom to practice these values elsewhere!

A Critique of Procedures and Strategies

A major part of Values Clarification is the set of recommended classroom exercises. These exercises, called "strategies," are really just questions to be used for discussing and "clarifying" values within the framework of the Values Clarification philosophy. They have been a major reason for the popularity of the approach, and even those educators aware of the substantive relativism of the Values Clarification theory have often used the exercises under the assumption that they are neutral tools with which to approach the topic of moral education. Yet even a cursory review of these materials reveals that this is clearly not the case.

Although I have not carefully evaluated each of the published 79 strategies in the latest VC handbook, it is possible to make some useful evaluative generalizations.[21]

First, the questions asked of the students and the supporting text *do* clearly betray the ideological biases of the VC theory. Moreover, the public discussion in the public school classroom of what have traditionally been regarded as very personal matters itself reflects a certain value bias. For example, the questions proposed for use with all ages include the following:

Would favor a law to limit families to two children?

Think we ought to legalize "pot" (marijuana)?

Approve of abortion?

Think the job of parenting should be shared by all adults?

Wouldn't mind having classes with no text-books?[22]

The following are questions typical of those recommended for secondary students and adults.[23]

Think giving grades in school inhibits meaningful learning?

Approve of premarital sex for boys? for girls?

Think sex education instruction in the schools should include techniques for lovemaking, contraception?

Would approve of a marriage between homosexuals being sanctioned by priest, minister, or rabbi?

Would approve of a young couple trying out marriage by living together for six months before actually getting married?

Would encourage legal abortion for an unwed daughter?

Would take your children to religious services even if they didn't want to go?

Would approve of contract marriages in which the marriage would come up for renewal every few years?

Would be upset if your daughter were living with a man who had no intentions of marriage? If your son were living with a woman, etc.?

Would be upset if organized religion disappeared?

Think the government should help support daycare centers for working mothers?

Think that parents should be subsidized to pick any school they want for their children?

Think we should legalize mercy killings?

It is not just that these questions reflect an extremely liberal social agenda; the very wording of the questions also suggests the favored response—one in line with such a philosophy or "world view." For example, when the values clarifiers want a positive answer they start a question with "approve" or "would approve"; when they want a negative answer they use other approaches, for example, "Would be upset if organized religion disappeared." The word *upset* suggests something negative and subtly implies that one should not be upset. And, of course, they don't propose the balancing questions, such as "Would be upset if public schools disappeared?"

Two other questions make this point in another way. Consider the item: "Think the government should *help support* daycare centers for working mothers?" Here the bias is toward yes. "Think that parents should be *subsidized* to pick any school they want for their children." Here the bias is toward no. In the first question tax money "helps support," but in the second tax money is called a "subsidy." For contrast, why not ask the question this way: "Do you think the government should restrict children to a public school rather than to the school the student freely chooses?" In short, the above questions show much bias, including the simple political bent toward supporting the growth of state-supported humanistic education while attacking any threat to their monopoly.

It does not take much imagination to think of questions which might be included if the authors were more positive to religion and religiously grounded values. As constituted, the VC materials have *no* questions about prayer, religious life, or religious virtues. Why not questions like: Do you pray often? Should you pray more? The VC authors urge the child to have pride in his position—but to love (agape), patience, humility, chastity, there is little or no reference. Furthermore, there is little about such virtues as cooperating with others, hard work, leadership, courage, and many other traditional values.

The same is true regarding the VC "strategies"—here is one discussed in an article by Bennett and Delattre:

In *Priorities,* Simon "asks you and your family at the dinner table, or your friends across the lunch table, to rank choices and to defend those choices in friendly discussion." One example of Simon's "delightful possibilities" for mealtime discussion is this:

Your husband or wife is a very attractive person. Your best friend is very attracted to him or her. How would you want them to behave?
  a. Maintain a clandestine relationship so you wouldn't know about it
  b. Be honest and accept the reality of the relationship
  c. Proceed with a divorce[24]

[This] exercise asks the student how he would want his spouse and best friend to behave if they were attracted to each other. Typically, the spouse and best friend are presented as having desires they will eventually satisfy anyway; the student is offered only choices that presuppose their relationship. All possibilities for self-restraint, fidelity, regard for others, or respect for mutual relationships and commitments are ignored.[25]

Finally, the mere presentation of numerous alternatives, with a clear bias in favor of "no right answer," has definite negative consequences on an immature mind, even if the traditional answer is one of the choices. The message students receive from the process itself is that values are all relative. (It is another case of the medium being the message.) Since conflicting positions are likely to be embodied by the student's peers, it is very hard to maintain a firm belief in absolute values without experiencing painful peer rejection and without having to reject one's classmates in return. It is hard enough for adults to reject a belief or behavior without also seeming to reject the person, and it is all the more difficult for impressionable children and adolescents.

Perhaps the most destructive aspect of Values Clarification, however, is the manner in which the public discussion of intimate family life undermines the authority of the father and mother. These exercises promote classroom discussion of everything from family rules about money, chores, and dating, to parental values and sanctions about masturbation, homosexuality, and premarital sex. In addition to violating the privacy of the family home, this often leads, as might be expected, to the alienation of children and their parents. Indeed, it appears that much of the angry and increasingly successful rejection of Values Clarification programs in public schools has come from parent's deep dismay over this issue—the public discussion of the properly private aspects of family life.[26]

Conclusion: An Unacceptable Theory

Since Values Clarification as a theory of moral education is based on a concept of complete innate goodness of the self, on the relativity (or nonexistence) of values, and on procedures which undermine the authority of the family, it is obviously unacceptable to traditional Christians and Jews.

Values Clarification denies the existence of God-given values (and implicitly of God as well) and claims that all opinions are of equal weight. It denies the basic Christian tenet of original sin and the Judeo-Christian obligation to struggle with evil, to name two of the more fundamental points of difference. And, of course, a duty to love, or a duty to fight injustice, like all duties, is likewise rejected.

But on the grounds of natural reason as well, the Values Clarification program should be rejected. The contradictions and incoherence of the system provide, in this writer's experience, one of the shallowest and intellectually most confused systems of thought yet contrived by the human mind. The wonder is that such an approach should ever have become so popular throughout American schools. In any case, the great success of Values Clarification points to the deep penetration of a confused moral relativism into the world of

American education and to the existence of a large group of naive American taxpayers who have done much to fund such views.

Whether "believers" or rationalists, parents and other taxpayers have every reason to reject the Values Clarification method of providing moral education to the next generation. That is, religious individuals and the best of the secular humanists—those I sometimes call "noble pagans"—both have equal cause for saying "no" to such an approach.

Kohlberg's Theory

Starting in the late 1950s Professor Lawrence Kohlberg (Harvard University) began developing a theory of the stages of moral growth which has become widely influential in educational and child psychology, and in the American public school system. Kohlberg's approach, as we will see, is also filled with ideological assumptions that make it a most useful example for observing the contemporary conflict between secular and Judeo-Christian morality.

General Background

Kohlberg's theory is based on the philosophy of John Dewey and the early work of Swiss psychologist Jean Piaget; but in his major concepts, methods, and applications Kohlberg has gone substantially beyond Dewey and Piaget to produce his own model of how moral reasoning develops in the child.[27] The basic research strategy has been to present moral dilemmas to children and young people and then to observe the reasons given for why one course of action should be followed rather than another. Kohlberg claims to have observed that the patterns of reasoning which people use are quite distinct and few in number; specifically, he has proposed that there are six stages or patterns of moral reasoning.

Before turning to these six stages, it should be noted that Kohlberg, like the VC theorists, is more interested in the form (or process) of moral reasoning than with the moral outcome, the actual decision made. Thus, two people may disagree about what is to be done but use the same kind of reasoning, or they may come to the same conclusion but for very different reasons. Like so many modern thinkers, Kohlberg becomes preoccupied with structure and changes in structure (process) while seemingly neglecting content.[28] However, as in the case of Values Clarification, moral relativism, while not explicitly defended, is nevertheless assumed by Kohlberg on the presuppositional level.

Kohlberg comes to far-reaching conclusions about the patterns of moral thought he claims to have observed. What he believes to have discovered is that when a person is studied over a number of years the evidence shows that he goes through a developmental series in the way he or she thinks about moral issues. Each pattern of moral reasoning in the sequence represents a qualitatively distinct "stage" in the person's moral development. Further, Kohlberg claims that the sequence of stages is the same for all people, although many never get to the higher stages. Since he proposes that there are six stages, this means that everyone develops morally by starting at stage 1 and over time proceeds in order from 2 to 6, unless growth stops at an intermediate stage. According to Kohlberg, nobody ever skips a stage and nobody ever regresses to an earlier stage. He does, however, allow for people to show a mixture of two adjacent stages, that is, a person can be in a transition between two stages. Briefly, Kohlberg's proposed stages of moral development are:

I. Preconventional Level

At this level the child is responsive to cultural rules and labels of good and bad, right or wrong, but interprets these labels in terms of either the physical or the hedonistic consequences of action (punishment, reward, exchange, or favors) or in terms of the physical power of those who enunciate the rules and labels. The level comprises the following two stages:

Stage 1: Punishment and obedience orientation. The physical consequences of action determine its goodness or badness regardless of the human meaning or value of these consequences. Avoidance of punishment and unquestioning deference to power are valued in their own right, not in terms of respect for an underlying moral order supported by punishment and authority (the latter being Stage 4).

Stage 2: Instrumental relativist orientation. Right action consists of that which instrumentally satisfies one's own needs and occasionally the needs of others. Elements of fairness, of reciprocity, and equal sharing are present, but they are always interpreted in a physical, pragmatic way. Reciprocity is a matter of "you scratch my back and I'll scratch yours," not of loyalty, gratitude, or justice.

II. Conventional Level

At this level, maintaining the expectations of the individual's family, group, or nation is perceived as valuable in its own right, regardless of immediate and obvious consequences. The attitude is one not only of *conformity* to personal expectations and social order, but of loyalty to it, of actively *maintaining,* supporting, and justifying the order and of identifying with the persons or groups involved in it. This level comprises the following two stages:

Stage 3: Interpersonal concordance or "good boy-nice girl" orientation. Good behavior is that which pleases or helps others and is approved by them. There is much conformity to stereotypical images of what is majority or "natural" behavior. Behavior is frequently judged by intention: "he means well" becomes important for the first time. One earns approval by being "nice."

Stage 4: "Law and order" orientation. There is orientation toward authority, fixed rules, and the maintenance of social behavior. Right behavior consists of doing one's duty, showing respect for authority, and maintaining the given social order for its own sake.

III. Post-Conventional, Autonomous, or Principled Level

At this level there is a clear effort to define moral values and principles that have validity and application apart from the authority of the groups of persons holding these principles and apart from the individual's own identification with these groups. This level again has two stages:

Stage 5: Social-contract legalistic orientation. Generally, this stage has utilitarian overtones. Right action tends to be defined in terms of general individual rights and in terms of standards that have been critically examined and agreed upon by the whole society. There is a clear awareness of the relativism of personal values and opinions and a corresponding emphasis on procedural rules for reaching consensus. Aside from what is constitutionally and democratically agreed upon, the right is a matter of personal "values" and "opinion." The result is an emphasis upon the "legal point of view," but with an emphasis upon the possibility of changing law in terms of rational consideration of social utility (rather than freezing it in terms of Stage 4, "law and order"). Outside the legal realm, free agreement and contract is the binding element of obligation. This is the "official" morality of the United States government and constitution.

Stage 6: Universal ethical-principle orientation. Right is defined by the decision of conscience in accord with self-chosen ethical principles appealing to logical comprehensiveness, universality, and consistency. These principles are abstract and ethical; they are not concrete moral rules like the Ten Commandments. At heart, these are universal principles of justice, of the reciprocity and equality of human rights and of respect for the dignity of human beings as individual persons.[29]

Empirical Critique

The first question we must ask—before moving to ideological bias—is whether the extensive research using and investigating Kohlberg's theory has generally supported the theory's main assumptions: first the existence of the six stages, and second the tendency over time for individuals to move from a lower to a higher stage and not to regress to a lower, earlier stage. This is not the place to go into a detailed summary of the very extensive research literature; instead I will present the main conclusions of various reviewers.[30]

1. The scale of moral development which consists of a set of moral dilemmas (Moral Maturity Scale) has not been standardized: i.e., the actual dilemmas used in the scale have not been fixed in number or in kind; the scoring procedure has been frequently revised, changed, and is often ambiguous.

To date (25 years after Kohlberg's approach was first published), the scoring manual still has not been published. As of October 1983, it is in press and should be available soon. Nevertheless, the scale's frequent revisions make many, perhaps most of the experiments prior to the publication of the scale no longer easily interpretable.

2. There is no evidence that scores on the Moral Development Scale can predict any kind of moral action. (Indeed, one study reports that activist students at Berkeley were predominantly either at Stage 6 or at Stage 2. These two very different stages of moral development lead to identical behavior.) This absence of concern with moral *behavior* is a natural conse-

quence of Kohlberg's exclusive focus on the reasoning given for a moral position. That certain actions may be "right" and others "wrong," substantively speaking, is ignored entirely. To make matters worse Kohlberg criticizes other approaches to moral education for receiving only modest support when tested against people's actual behavior. But he refuses to allow the tough behavioral test to be applied to his model— because his approach is concerned only with thought—not action.

3. The evidence offered in support of the idea that the sequence of stages is invariable has revealed no clear support for this position, and the cross-cultural data on early development provides almost no support for qualitative differences between stages, or for their fixed order.

Lockwood's recent summary of the evidence for Kohlberg's stages, which evaluated those studies that tried to show that student moral maturity scores can be improved, is noteworthy.[31] Lockwood found that in classes in which instructors frequently illustrated reasoning at a stage just above that expressed by the student or group there was a very modest increase in Kohlberg stage level. That is, after many periods of direct discussions, scores on Kohlberg's scale reliably "advanced," at least according to some of the studies, by about a third of a stage. As Lockwood concluded, all that these studies show is that where students are directly stimulated to discuss morality in Kohlbergian terms, there is evidence that the students after some weeks of these classes will express themselves in Kohlbergian terminology. Any teacher familiar with the adeptness with which students learn to regurgitate the favored view in a particular class will hardly find in such a conclusion much support for Kohlberg's elaborate theory of moral development.

Even Kohlberg himself appears to be having second thoughts about his theory, although it continues to enjoy wide influence. He recently conceded, for example, that stage regression may occur.

Pointing out that none of his longitudinal subjects had achieved stage six by 1976, Kohlberg lamented at a recent symposium: "Perhaps all the sixth-stage persons of the 1960s had been wiped out, perhaps they had regressed, or maybe it was all my imagination in the first place."[32]

Kohlberg later conceded—after a recent longitudinal study in America and Turkey in which Stage 6 did not occur at all—that maybe the problem was not *regression,* but that Stage 6 did not exist:

This result (that is, the failure to find a Stage 6) indicated that my sixth stage was mainly a theoretical construction suggested by the writings of "elite" figures like Martin Luther King, not an empirically confirmed developmental construct. . . . We now think the safest interpretation would be to view the construct of a sixth stage as representing an elaboration of the B (or advanced) substage of Stage 5.[33]

Many psychologists share similar doubts regarding the empirical support for Kohlberg's theory. Professor Robert Hogan of Johns Hopkins quite flatly states that there is *no* evidence that Kohlberg's stages exist.[34] Of course, different patterns of moral reasoning or explanation exist, but the evidence for stage sequence, especially with respect to the higher stages, does not exist, according to Hogan. Hogan bases his position partly on the fact, still true as of late 1983, that Kohlberg's scale for measuring stages has not met the necessary standard of reliability, validity, etc., to justify *any* conclusions about stage existence, much less the order of supposed natural development. Hogan also bases his criticism on evidence from his own research that strongly suggests, for example, that the difference between Stage 5 and Stage 6 individuals is a difference in personality type. To claim that it is a difference in the *level* of moral maturity is, Hogan argues, simply a scientifically unacceptable expression of Kohlberg's own political (and social) beliefs.

In fact, one of the central errors in Kohlberg's system is the tendency to allow the content of moral reasoning to influence his scoring system. That is, the stages are supposed to reflect how a person reasons about moral issues but not what the person thinks. To allow content to influence the way a stage is scored introduces particular values disguised as cognitive structure and completely undermines the legitimacy of the system. Detailed evidence that this problem is widespread in Kohlberg's scoring system can be found in a recent thesis of Thomas Kalam (1981).[35] Kalam, who worked directly with Kohlberg, comes to the conclusion that this very serious problem turns Kohlberg's stages into conceptually and empirically nonexistent stages.

In conclusion, the empirical support for Kohlberg's model is very tenuous at best, and although the issue is still an active one, at present the system is beleaguered. One prominent researcher, Prof. Joseph Adelson of the University of Michigan, commented, "I suspect the system (of Kohlberg) is beginning to fall apart."[36] Kohlberg himself describes his model as a "leaky boat" which requires much patching and which may sink.[37]

Ideological Critique

The most recent and powerful attacks on Kohlberg, all from secular social scientists, have focused on the political and ideological assumptions—the doctrine—embedded in this theory of moral development. The most important of these have been the critiques by Sullivan (1977)[38] and by Hogan and Emler (1978).[39] I will present this analysis in some detail, leaning more heavily on the work of the latter two psychologists. Their critique is particularly significant because it goes beyond Kohlberg's theory of moral development and generally reflects the growing awareness within social science that truly neutral or objective theory is a philosophical impossibility. This collapse of the implicit assumption of objectivity among social scientists has profound and encouraging implications for the use of Judeo-Christian beliefs and values in alternative models of moral development. If neither is, in any meaningful sense, "values neutral," then many of the modernist objections to a "religious" model should lose their force— at least with open-minded academics and public policymakers.

Very generally, Hogan and Emler see Kohlberg's theory as an expression of liberal ideology. Specifically, they charge it with containing three major assumptions which Kohlberg has not examined or even made explicit, assumptions of an intrinsically ideological nature.

The first assumption is that of *rationalism*. For Kohlberg, moral development is an entirely cognitive process. He is concerned only with setting up abstract moral problems or dilemmas which pit various rather abstract principles against each other. His intent is to focus reasoning on a choice between two different moral priciples, in such a way that the person's criteria for the choice are revealed. The concern is with getting rational argument from the person—argument or reasons that defend his choice. Thus, as already noted, Kohlberg's position totally ignores moral action. Equally problematic is Kohlberg's neglect of the will (to resist temptation, for example), as well as the profound emotional and interpersonal elements involved in all natural moral dilemmas. For Kohlberg, the Cartesian "I think, therefore I am" is the *sine qua non* of the human moral situation. Kohlberg's use of highly abstract and often contrived moral dilemmas is one expression of this extreme rationalism. Again, however, Kohlberg himself may be rethinking the excessively rationalistic nature of his theory, having described his own work as proposing "science fiction" dilemmas.[40]

The second assumption is that of *individualism,* which Kohlberg assumes is the natural direction of moral development. That is, he assumes that morality develops toward internalized moral controls in which the individual is socially and morally autonomous. Each individual is presumed to be able to ultimately discover for himself a natural morality that owes nothing to any cultural, historical, or religious heritage. Any approach to moral education which begins with presumed virtues (such as in Christianity and Judaism) is disparaged as reflecting a backward "bag of virtues" mentality.

Thus, Kohlberg simply assumes, without discussion, that obedience to the self—to one's internal code—is superior to obedience to God or submission to a higher moral order. The nature of this self is not described or explicitly discussed by Kohlberg, but he appears to assume, as do the VC theorists, that it is intrinsically entirely good, and thus, that there is no natural human tendency to evil. This self-conscious ignoring of the problem of evil is enough by itself to make Kohlberg's theory untenable as a model of moral "development." Kohlberg assumes there is no natural tendency for humans to exploit, hurt, and oppress—except possibly for those people still at Stages 1 and 2. And even here it is the result of inadequate cognitive functioning. What Kohlberg never addresses is the sad frequency of human exploitation and hurtful selfishness—something often done by very cognitively advanced people and societies.

A third assumption is that of *liberalism*. Hogan and Emler describe Kohlberg's Stage 6, with its concern for justice, as an expression of Kohlberg's personal philosophy. They identify the moral philosophies of Kant, Hare, and especially John Rawls as influencing Kohlberg here. It is beyond the present scope to engage in a detailed analysis of liberal moral philosophy, but this much should be obvious: whatever moral philosophy one adopts, liberal or otherwise, one must acknowledge it, describe it, and defend it. One cannot just imply that one's personal philosophy is the pure scientific expression of how human nature spontaneously develops when it grows to its highest stage! This appears to be, in essence, precisely what Professor Kohlberg has done. (An especially strong critique of Kohlberg's misuse of liberal philosophy is noted by Levin.[41])

Apparently, it is not just Kohlberg's critics who have been disturbed by his tendency to mix his personal beliefs and values with the supposed neutral processes of moral development. Once again, Kohlberg himself—after twenty years of insisting on neutrality in moral education—has finally changed his position by writing that the moral stage concept is valuable for research purposes, but:

> It is not a sufficient guide to the moral educator, who deals with concrete morality in a school world in which value content as well as structure, behavior as well as reasoning, must be dealt with. In this context, an educator must be a socializer, teaching value content and behavior, not merely a Socratic or Rogerian process-facilitator of development. In becoming a socializer and advocate, the teacher moves into "indoctrination," a step that I originally believed to be invalid both philosophically and psychologically. I thought indoctrination invalid philosophically because the value content taught was culturally and personally relative, and because teaching value content was a violation of the child's rights. I thought indoctrination invalid psychologically because it could not lead to meaningful structural change.
>
> I no longer hold these negative views of indoctrinative moral education, and I now believe that the concepts guiding moral education must be partly "indoctrinative."[42]

One final ideological bias in Kohlberg, not mentioned by Hogan and Emler but perhaps most significant of all, is his functional *atheism*. This assumption lies behind Kohlberg's favoring of individual autonomy and explains his consistently placing answers giving a religious rationale at Stage 4 or lower. As mentioned, he *assumes* that any reasoning based on the acceptance of authority, human or divine, derives from rules, not from principles. Consider the following example from Kohlberg's explanation of his scoring system, which is characteristic. The respondent, a boy named Richard, was asked for his moral reaction to mercy killing. He replied:

> I don't know. In one way, it's murder; it's not a right or a privilege of man to decide who shall live and who should die. God put life into everybody on earth and you're taking away something from that person that came directly from God, and you're destroying something that is very sacred; it's in a way part of God and it's almost destroying a part of God when you kill a person. There's something of God in everyone.

Kohlberg comments:

> Here Richard clearly displays a Stage 4 concept of life as sacred in terms of its place in a categorical moral or religious order. The value of human life is universal, it is true for all humans. It is still, however, dependent on something else, upon respect for God and God's authority; it is not an autonomous human value.[43]

Kohlberg simply assumes that the culturally determined principle of "an autonomous human value" and of obedience to the self is higher than one based on the free choice of obedience to God. Thus does his scoring system express—and expose—his ideology. Belief in the sacredness of life and obedience to God is to Kohlberg not qualitatively different from Archie Bunker's defense of lower-middle-class American law and order. Both get scored as conventional Stage 4 morality.

Conclusion

Values Clarification and Kohlberg's model are the two most influential theories of moral development operating in the

United States today. However, it would be a mistake to assume that the removal of these egregious examples of publicly supported moral subjectivism would suffice to solve the ethical problems of modern American society. Although exposing "the myth of values neutrality" surrounding such liberal secular ideology is itself a desirable end, our efforts must go much further than that or, as in the biblical parable, we may find "seven worse demons" coming in to fill the void. First, our arguments must not be directed exclusively at this or that theory. Rather, we must make our case at the presuppositional level, and this requires something of a developed "world view." Those with traditional beliefs and values must learn to identify faulty *assumptions*—whether about the nature of man, the existence of higher law, the role of families in the formation of character, or a host of other basic issues. Second, those who object to secular, relativistic approaches to the teaching of moral values must do more than just complain. Alternate theories and models must be developed, proposed, and supported in the marketplace of ideas. Thoughtful alternate programs and textbooks must be developed. Parents must be concerned enough about the education of their children to become intimately involved in the process, something which can require great personal sacrifice. And finally, religious believers should be most careful not to make the same rationalist mistake of assuming that morals are mere cognitive commitments. We all know it is usually not so hard to *know* what is good—the hard part is to *do* it. The moral life is a *way of life,* made possible by God's grace and involving all that man is: intellect, heart (emotions), and will. Let us pray that future generations will be given every opportunity to choose this way of life for themselves.

EIGHT

Trends in State Regulation of Religious Schools

William B. Ball

Where benevolent planning, armed with political and economic power, becomes wicked is when it tramples on peoples' rights for the sake of their own good. —*C.S. Lewis*

As an attorney who has often been in court in cases involving constitutional liberties associated with education, I have become increasingly aware of the interest of great numbers of Americans in real educational freedom. That freedom is a freedom to express and to receive ideas. It is the freedom of parents to choose a particular education for their children. It is the freedom of churches to found educational ministries for children and to be in control of these ministries, once founded.

The First, Ninth, and Fourteenth Amendments to the American Constitution protect that cluster of freedoms, and the state constitutions, if observed, likewise do.

Educational freedom, however, is threatened today by a single gross presumption. That presumption was a favorite idea of Otto von Bismarck, and it has been the very foundation of the modern totalitarian state: *that the state is the sole or superior educator.*

To the extent it is given actual effect, such a presumption will extinguish all that is comprehended by the term "educational freedom." It is not hard to see how. Government, using its taxing powers, first creates a system of schools which, by reason of their philosophic, non-religious, moral, or quality characteristics, may not be conscientiously acceptable to all citizens. Then it creates truancy laws containing criminal sanctions which require all children either to attend those schools—or to attend non-government schools. But under the presumption that the state is the sole or superior educator, non-government schools must be under government control. They may, at a particular moment, enjoy a measure of freedom—but because of the presumption, it is freedom on a leash, the leash firmly held by government.

It follows, as night follows day, that all the basic elements of education must ultimately reflect whatever government administrators deem to be sound "public policy," what *they* feel the needs and dispositions of the populace should be, and how *they* think a "competent" citizenry is best formed. Those elements necessarily embrace curriculum, teacher qualification, teaching methodology, and textbooks. And flowing from them is the inevitable fulfillment of the prediction of Benjamin Disraeli, in his 1839 criticism of the attempt to place English education in the hands of the governmental bureaucracy: ". . . All children would be thrown into the same mint, and all would come out with the same impress and superscription."[2]

Of course, if government knows best, then it *should* control all education—that is, if it knows best what is moral, knows best what is wise, knows best the human mind and spirit, knows best what is good for children, knows best how learning takes place. But if government *thinks* it knows best, it should cease the pretense that its interest is only in minimal oversight of religious and other private alternatives to government schools.

Supporters of non-government education do accept the idea that some statutes, limited and rational, affecting schools are necessary in the name of the common good. A reasonable fire, safety, building, or sanitary ordinance, or a statute imposing those few universally agreed-to "basics" (English, mathematics, civics, etc.) give rise to no objections. But statutes which install the government education bureaucracy as the ultimate supervisor of, and prescriber for, all non-government education do indeed occasion the profoundest of concerns.[3]

Under these statutes, the citizen desiring educational freedom stands at a Y in the road. One fork of the Y leads into public education which, in conscience, he may reject. The other leads into "private" education which may be just another branch of public education, "private" only in the sense that its sponsors must pay for it while the government runs it.

That is not educational freedom.

What I have just described is not mere theory, guesswork, or exaggeration. It is certainly not an attempt to sow needless fears. Rather, I have described realities of which everyone should be taking cognizance.

Proceeding up the first fork of the Y—into America's public schools—I scarcely need comment upon one aspect of educational liberty: the right of children to receive quality education in the basics. The recent Report of the National Commission on Excellence in Education,[4] and a tidal wave of other unimpeachable criticism,[5] including the perceptive recent statement of Admiral Rickover,[6] make clear that the government educational system cannot be relied upon as a quality alternative to nonpublic education.[7] Another aspect of educational liberty necessarily relates to the moral domain, to discipline and order, to the inculcating of civic virtue. Many parents rightly believe that they cannot today in conscience place their children in public schools due to a widespread lack, in those schools, of a tranquil, morally nurturing social and learning environment.

Finally, government schools, by operation of Supreme Court decisions, are required to be antiseptically free of religion. It is inadequate for apologists for the Supreme Court to point out that, in its decision banning Bible-reading and prayers in public schools, the Court nevertheless said that comparative religion could still be studied, or the Bible "for its literary and historic qualities."[8] Those tolerances may satisfy some, but such an arm's length approach to religion is offensive to many persons of profound religious faith. They regard comparative religion as an abomination, and the teaching of the Bible other than as the Word of God as sacrilegious. In terms of educational freedom, the question is not, "What is belief to the secularist?" but *"What is belief to the believer and how is that belief expressed?"* The cold but legal answer is that those beliefs and those expressions must be stiff-armed out of public education.

For millions of parents, therefore, the public education fork of the Y is a roadway that cannot conscientiously be taken. What about the second fork of the Y? It is this fork of the road, both in many states and at the federal level, which is increasingly threatened with closure.

At the federal level, the Supreme Court, on May 24, 1983,[9] held that the tax-exempt status of every nonpublic school in the nation shall depend on its conformity to a super-law of unknown and unknowable dimension—a law above the Constitution—vaguely described as "federal public policy." Waiting in the wings are significant forces seeking to extend this undefined condition to the nation's nonpublic schools. Schools which partake of no federal funding whatever, but which merely exercise the traditional liberty of being for boys only, or for girls only, for example, appear to be targeted for loss of tax-exempt status. And there are churches which are now being told that their schools must recruit students and faculty *solely* on a racial basis, and not according to religious conviction, or else be taxed. What is next? Affirmative action to recruit teachers or students whose "sexual preference" is homosexual? In any event, a giant step backwards in federal civil rights is now being taken: the taxation of religion and the resulting coercion of religion to lock-step itself with the dubious aims of secular government policymakers.

At the state level there are equally threatening developments. These bring to the fore the most significant existing aspect of the question of the governance of education—an aspect of that question which I would submit is of even greater importance than, say, the relationship between federal agencies and public school districts.

The unhappy fact is that, in all too many of the states, State Education Boards or State Education Departments are aggressively seeking to control nonpublic schools. But these are schools which the state did not found and does not fund. By and large, as I have noted, these schools are amenable to certain statutes, such as reasonable compulsory attendance laws. But they will not agree that state educational bureaucracies shall license them, supervise them, decide what they will teach, who will teach it, and how things shall be taught. When the state education officials seek to impose their recipes for education on private schools, many of those schools have stated in court, with splendid candor, that they do not see the government schools as particularly desirable models. And when the state educators warn judges of the great disadvantage to children which will result if the state's educational mandates are not followed, the embarrassing question inevitably arises: Are the public schools, with *100 percent* governmental control, succeeding in producing high-grade education?

The scope of the current problem is perhaps best illustrated by examining some actual situations recently in our courts in which the issue has been the governance of private education.

Mainly, the schools involved have been religious schools. There have been, for example, the Roman Catholic schools in Philadelphia, Chicago, and Scranton, which were confronted with a bold power play by the National Labor Relations Board seeking to intrude itself upon the church as though the church were a shipping company and its employees dock hands. Happily, after three federal courts denied NLRB jurisdiction over these ministries of the church, the Supreme Court held that the Congress never intended such schools to be within the purview of the National Labor Relations Act.

Amish, Mennonite, fundamentalist, and evangelical schools have all been forced into court to protect their right to exist. These cases have brought to the fore three features of the "governance" problem:

1. *Vagueness* v. *Clarity in Regulatory Laws.* Just now the effort is being made by the State of Michigan to shut down schools operated by two fundamentalist Christian churches—excellent schools whose students achieve well in nationally standardized achievement tests and which are supported 100 percent by the congregations which founded the schools (and without one cent of state aid or the benefit of any state programs).[10] The schools are the enthusiastic choice of mature, intelligent, and caring parents. The state says it must extinguish these marvelous voluntary enterprises because state statutes require it to. But the Michigan statutes which the state cites are wonderfully confusing. They provide, for example, that the courses of study in a nonpublic school must be "of the same standard as provided by the general school laws of the state." But the "general school laws of the state" say nothing about "standards." Upon trial we thought it would be of interest to find out what state officials themselves thought "standards" means. Some said it means "quality," others said it means "courses," others said it means the specific courses of "math, science, English and social studies," while yet another said it means just "government and civics." In other words, as

the Supreme Court said in a leading case on statutory vagueness, here was terminology "wholly lacking in 'terms susceptible of objective measurements' . . . Men of common intelligence must necessarily guess at its meaning and differ as to its application . . ."[11] Yet on the thin pretext of this and other equally vague statutory language, two fine religious schools in Michigan are threatened with shut-down.

Or take this interesting example from regulations sought to be imposed in Kentucky. In 1977, the Kentucky State Board of Education decided to inaugurate criminal prosecutions in every county of the state in which a parent had a child enrolled in a non-state-licensed school. Standard IV of the Standards for Accrediting Kentucky Schools required compliance with the following mandate (and state officials emphasized that it was indeed a mandate):

Curriculum objectives, decisions, and implementations should be characterized by unit, balance, and articulation with the schools below and above it, while retaining flexibility.

The pastor of a Christian school testified that he was not able to understand this language. Naturally. Nobody could. Yet parents were to be jailed because their schools were not found in compliance with it.

Sometimes State Education Boards, while busy hounding pastors, schoolmasters, and parents who don't think that state controls assure quality, themselves betray lack of literacy. Hear, for example, the language of Standard VI of the same Kentucky "Standards":

Major safeguards for quality education are a well-designed master schedule, effective administrative routines, adequate undisturbed class time, and *profusion* for a high degree of self-direction on the part of students. (Emphasis supplied. "And profusion" was not a misprint.)

The unhappy fact is that a very large number of state statutes conferring regulatory powers on state agencies over private schools are unconstitutionally vague, or are overbroad, or constitute limitless (and other void) delegations of legislative power. And when we turn to the regulatory work product of many of the agencies, the picture is worse. Occasionally the problem (as in Kentucky) is a simple failure to have mastered English. But mostly the problem has to do with a seemingly profound compulsion of a number of state bureaucracies to multiply their controls over all education.

Here, one would think that restraint and modesty would prevail: have not those state education bureaucracies something of a challenge to get *their own* houses in order? Some states—while faced with a failing public education system, supported by taxpayers in a time of economic distress have nonetheless expended vast sums and enormous energy on court cases attacking Christian congregations which have been interested enough in education as to have established good schools—indeed schools which save local taxpayers $600 to $100 per pupil per year!

2. *Governmental Prescriptions* v. *"Proof in the Pudding."* In the principal court cases in which state education agencies have sought to close down nonpublic schools, the schools have completely shown the good *results* they are achieving educationally. They challenge the state agencies and say: "Are you, in the government schools, producing such good results?" But the state authorities duck this question and instead protest: "We have the *recipe* for good education. Follow our recipe, and good education inevitably results. Fail to follow it, and bad education results. Since you fail to follow our prescription, you will be educating badly, and therefore, for the sake of children, you must be shut down."

Thus in these cases the state's argument has been limited to insisting on its recipe, while the schools have insisted that "the proof is in the pudding." As Dr. Donald Erickson, of the University of California at Los Angeles, recognized by the

Supreme Court as an educational expert, has so strongly insisted: "The test of education is simply this: has learning resulted?" And that is simply unanswerable common sense.

But state boards and departments seem unfazed by this rather elementary consideration. Instead they push doggedly ahead, brandishing the recipe and oblivious of the pudding.

The recipe typically involves at least three matters: (1) state certification of nonpublic school teachers, (2) state prescription of curriculum and, (3) school licensing.

The pretext for teacher certification is the argument that it assures quality teaching. The argument has a plausible ring. Do we not require doctors to be certified? electricians? lawyers? But well established by expert educational testimony in litigation in Ohio, Kentucky, Maine, and Michigan (in all of which states such certification has been required) is the fact that teacher certification does *not* assure good teaching; further, teaching involves no such knowledge base as is found in medicine—or the statutes and case precedents which are the knowledge base of law. One educational scholar, Russell Kirk, has pointed to those factors in teaching which *do* give assurance that learning will take place: possession of talent, the "teaching knack," literacy, a good general cultural background, and—importantly—love of children and an even sacrifical dedication to teaching them. And it is those characteristics of teachers with which nonpublic schools—especially the religious schools—abound. It is inconceivable that schools which can be shown to provide good teaching could—as in Nebraska—be *shut down* because their teachers did not hold state licenses.

As to state prescription of curriculum, it is important to note that in those cases which have come into the courts, no nonpublic schools challenge state statutes which require the old "common branches of learning"—English, mathematics, civics, history, geography, etc.—the universally accepted core of "basics." These schools do, however, challenge placing in the hands of state boards or departments blank check powers to prescribe curriculum. The schools—especially the religious schools—deeply resent efforts of state agencies to impose value-loaded curricular items on them, and their proper sense of independence rejects the notion that a state agency shall have power to impose curriculum on non-state-funded schools. From curriculum imposition all too logically comes content prescription and textbook prescription.

The great catch-all prescription area is school licensing. A license is a permit to exist. Since the American tradition rejects the licensing of First Amendment activities, state licensing laws are sometimes given labels such as "approval," "certification," "chartering," or "accreditation." Call it what they will, it is still licensing—or permission to exist. Especially do religious schools reject licensing. In recent cases involving fundamentalist Christian schools, pastors—fully willing to face jail for their beliefs—have clearly insisted that they cannot seek a license from the state in order to carry out a church ministry. Constitutionally they are correct. The Supreme Court has held the church-school to be "an integral part of the religious mission" of the sponsoring church.[12] It has also held that licenses may not be imposed upon the exercise of religious ministries.[13]

Apart from the central vice of licensing of First Amendment activities, the licensing statutes inevitably vest accordion-like discretionary powers in the state bureaucracy—which is then free to impose a vast range of conditions to be met before the license can be had. In the *Whisner* case[14] in Ohio, before the Ohio Supreme Court commendably held its action unconstitutional, the Ohio State Board of Education published a volume entitled, *Minimum Standards for Ohio Elementary Schools.* This "minimum" consisted of 90-odd requirements addressing every conceivable facet of a school's existence—even one "standard" (No. 401-02[o]) which boldly recited:

All activities shall conform to policies adopted by the State Board of Education.

In these state prescriptions we see vivid examples of how state prescriptive measures violate educational freedom.[15]

3. *Compelling State Interest* v. *Entanglement.* So far as religious schools (now being harassed in a number of states) are concerned, this third feature of the "governance problem" needs brief comment. The Supreme Court has long held that, in order for government to limit the exercise of a First Amendment liberty, there must be a supreme societal interest at stake, or, in the Court's phrasing, a "compelling state interest."[16] But the Supreme Court has also held that the Establishment clause of the First Amendment prohibits "excessive entanglements" between government and religious bodies—in particular, church-schools.[17] The Court has told us that "entanglement" means such things as "continuing day-to-day relationships" between government and church, or "sustained and detailed administrative relationships for enforcement of statutory or administrative standards."

Now state education agencies, to justify imposing their regulatory schemes on private schools, vigorously insist that these regulations are a life-or-death matter. They argue that a supreme societal interest—the well-being of children—will be sacrificed if the regulations are not imposed. Thus the states push hard indeed to convince courts that unless the schools and teachers are state-licensed and the curriculum state-dictated, education itself is threatened, children are doomed, and our society is in the gravest jeopardy.

However, the state must also prove that its regulatory scheme will not cause "excessive entanglements between government and church-schools." The church-state separation principle is strongly expressed in the "excessive entanglement" ban. To prove *this* point, the state now typically contradicts all that it says about a "compelling state interest." It speaks of its regulatory scheme as merely "minimal." The state says that it has no purpose to involve itself in the church-school. It has no desire to exercise surveillance or monitoring of the school. It is not concerned about course content or the textbooks used, or how teachers perform. The government now appears neutral, aloof, benign, non-intrusive.

The courts, we may hope, will recognize that government cannot have it both ways with the religious schools. If there *is* a supreme societal interest in imposing the regulations, then it follows that government *must* entangle itself in the school— get into the classroom, monitor the teachers, prescribe the textbooks, dictate the course content. But if, to avoid such flatly unconstitutional entanglements, it does *not* do those things, but suffers the school to select, for example, its own course content and its own textbooks, then the state's claim of compelling state interest vanishes as the pretense it truly is.

In our age of looking to the government to protect us from all manner of evil or plain inconvenience, the question must arise: If government education agencies are *not* permitted to control private education, what protection has the public against shoddy education or fly-by-night schools? I believe the answers to be as follows:

First, there is the parent market. I find myself in agreement with Milton Friedman's constructive views with respect to the ability of parents to choose, and choose well, if they are but permitted to. In most private school litigation in which I have been involved, the parents have been people willing to sacrifice financially for a private school education. This, in the face of high taxation, inflation, and sometimes job loss. Education is a very demanding market. The parents care for their children and closely monitor what they are receiving in the school. As mature heads of families often with very responsible positions, they are quite capable of judging whether the education is of good quality—far better, in fact, than the state bureaucracy. Parents *will* withdraw their children from schools which are poor in quality or poor in discipline. That in fact is why so many parents *have* removed their children from public schools.

Secondly, we must ask again: Are those schools which are totally state-operated and totally state-funded today producing high-grade education and a young citizenry well grounded in civic virtue? Certainly not generally. That leads great numbers of Americans to conclude that they will prefer to put their faith in nonpublic schools rather than in a bureaucracy which really has no proper business involving itself in institutions not its own.

Thirdly, criminal and other laws of the states offer much protection to the public. I am thinking here of laws against fraud, embezzlement, false solicitation, and child abuse, and of fire, safety, sanitation, and building laws.

Finally, we must put into the balance the two factors here competing for the governance of schools: the completely unsupported case in favor of government control of nonpublic education as contrasted with the supreme need to protect constitutional freedom in education. That freedom will not be safe until the governance of private education is placed securely in the hands of the governors of higher education—the parents, churches, and other voluntary associations whose sacrificial initiatives have brought us the blessings of these schools in the first place.

NINE

Pluralism and the Limits of Neutrality

Francis Canavan, S.J.

THE UNITED STATES IS A PLURALIST SOCIETY. That is a commonplace and is taken as stating the problem to which the American relation between religion and the law is supposed to furnish the solution. The general principle of that relationship is an official governmental neutrality among all creeds, one that respects all beliefs but grants no favor to any of them. The name of the game is pluralism and the rules of the game can be summed up in one word: neutrality.

James Madison gave classic expression to a view of pluralism as essentially a constructive force in the most famous of the Federalist Papers, no. 10, during the campaign for the ratification of the newly proposed Constitution of the United States in 1787. First, he argued, the division of society into "factions" is inevitable, and the more inevitable the more developed a society becomes. Since we cannot avoid having factions, a large number of them is desirable, according to Madison, because they will serve as checks and balances against one another, preventing any particular party or point of view from becoming dominant.

Madison quietly assumes, however, that the pluralism in our society will not be too pronounced. Prone though men are to use power unjustly, well though we "know that neither moral nor religious motives can be relied on as an adequate control" on this propensity,[1] Madison nonetheless takes it for granted that, at least on sober second thought, the bulk of the American people will agree that there are rationally discernible norms of justice, that people do have valid rights, and that some "projects" are "improper or wicked." Underlying the pluralism there is a *consensus juris,* an agreement about justice and right, sufficient to keep pluralism from tearing the nation apart.

It is on this very point, however, that Madison has been criticized in one of the minor classics of twentieth-century American political theory, Robert A. Dahl's *A Preface to Democratic Theory.* Professor Dahl is one of the most distinguished members of the school of political scientists known, if only to their critics, as "pluralists." Madison's argument rests, he says, on the idea of natural rights, a foundation that traditionalists would heartily affirm. For Professor Dahl, however, this is Madison's irremediable flaw: "the logic of natural rights seems to require a transcendental view in which the right is 'natural' because God directly or indirectly wills it. . . . such an argument inevitably involves a variety of assumptions that at best are difficult and at worst impossible to prove to the satisfaction of anyone of positivist or skeptical predispositions."[2]

Dahl, therefore, shifts his own essentially Madisonian model of democratic government from the foundation of natural right and justice and bases it on the equality of all preferences. He proposes "to lay down political equality as an end to be maximized, that is, to postulate that the goals of every adult citizen of a republic are to be accorded equal value in determining governmental policies."[3] Madison relied on pluralism to prevent the tyranny of the majority and did not think he was talking nonsense; to him the term, tyranny, was meaningful as a violation of natural rights. Dahl, since he finds natural rights (or any principle of natural justice) highly dubious, lays down a postulate. The goals of every adult citizen are to be accorded equal value, not because they have any value at all which reason could discern, but because, in the absence of any rational standard for comparing them, we stipulate that all adult values are equal.

The views of a single political scientist may not in themselves be of great significance. But Dahl gives scholarly expression to what is now the dominant view in articulate public opinion. We are now to be protected, in this view, not from tyranny but from the imposition of anyone's or any group's values on anyone else. No opinion and no policy can be regarded as legitimate which threatens to conflict with this supreme norm of "our pluralistic society." It is uncommitted not only to any particular religious beliefs but to any particular moral principles as well.

Liberal government therefore is understood to be neutral government. But to make this assertion only raises the question: neutral about what? The answer to that question turns out to be itself a political and even a moral issue. Professor Dahl's answer is that government should be neutral about matters that belong in the area of Autonomous Decisions. But this itself only begs the question, for as Dahl further explains:

Judgments as to the appropriate domain of Autonomous Decisions are constantly changing. Efforts to define the domain once and for all have always failed. Thus in the United States, owning and driving a machine that emits exhaust fumes is rapidly moving out of the domain of Autonomous Decisions to regulation by collective decision . . . , while sexual practices among consenting adults are moving from collective regulation to the domain of individual choice.[4]

What belongs in the area of Autonomous Decisions is, therefore, a question that requires a public and political decision. In making such a decision the people, through their representatives, take a public stand on what they will leave to individual choice and what they will subject to legal regulation. Leaving a matter to individual choice is as much a public decision as deciding to regulate it and implies some public scheme of values quite as much as a decision to regulate does.

In practice, of course, the controversy over a question of this kind gets such settlement as it does get through a political process in which expediency and rhetoric play a large part. Slogans such as "You can't legislate morality" and "No group has a right to impose its morality on others" are freely used. If at all possible, the First Amendment is invoked on the absolute necessity of separating church and state. In fact, however, the size and (perhaps even more important) the financial power of the groups involved, and the importance that both sides attach to the values at stake, have more to do with the way in which the dispute is settled than does any appeal to principle.

Taking a historical example may better serve to illustrate how this process has traditionally worked. The American people in the nineteenth century felt few qualms about banning polygamy throughout the United States, even though John Stuart Mill had warned them against doing so in Utah. Since Mormons had exiled themselves to a remote and previously uninhabited territory in order to practice polygamy, he said, "it is difficult to see on what principles but those of tyranny they can be prevented from living there under what laws they please, provided they commit no aggression on other nations and allow perfect freedom of departure to those who are dissatisfied with their ways."[5] But the Mormons were few in number and without influence, while on the other hand monogamy was solidly embedded in the religious and moral beliefs of the great majority of Americans.

The U.S. Supreme Court, as is fitting in a First Amendment case, found a secular and political reason for upholding the federal law against the practice of polygamy in the territories. The Court declared that "polygamy leads to the patriarchal principle, and . . . when applied to large communities, fetters the people in stationary despotism, while the principle cannot long exist in connection with monogamy."[6] The ban on polygamy, in other words, was alleged to strike a blow for political liberty. One may suspect, however, that the Court was in fact reflecting the moral conscience of the people at large.

Conversely, one may suspect that if the polygamous minority were not so small—if, say, 45 percent of Americans believed in polygamy and many of them wanted to practice it—the Supreme Court would today find polygamy to be in the domain of Autonomous Decisions or, as the Court prefers to put it, to be included in the right of privacy. The court would of course also have to try to gauge the feelings of the 55 percent majority who still objected to polygamy. How strong are their feelings? Will the majority swallow a flat declaration that prohibiting polygamy is beyond the constitutional powers of government? Or must we take a more gradual approach by finding one anti-polygamy statute after another vague and overbroad while maintaining that in principle government may regulate polygamy? These would be difficult questions to answer. But one way or another, the Court, along with the other agencies of government, would search for a means of taking the divisive issue of polygamy out of politics.

The reason for doing so would be the practical one of lessening social and political strife. The principled justification for doing it, however, would be the neutrality among conflicting beliefs to which government is committed in a liberal society. But the justification would only raise once again the questions of the matters about which government ought to be neutral, how far it should go in the quest for neutrality, and to what extent neutrality is ultimately possible.

It is an old half-truth that you cannot legislate morality. The other and more significant half of the truth is that a society's laws inevitably reflect its morals and its religion. As a society's religious and moral beliefs change, then, so will its laws.

This thought powerfully impressed the mind of a noted Victorian writer, Sir James Fitzjames Stephen. He gave prophetic expression to it in his *Liberty, Equality, Fraternity,* which was published in 1873. In this book Stephen foretold, a century ago, the legal-moral issues of our day, because he saw their causes in the changes of religious belief taking place in his day.

Stephen wrote the book as a critique of John Stuart Mill's famous essay *On Liberty.* But R.J. White, who edited a new printing of *Liberty, Equality, Fraternity* for the Cambridge University Press in 1967, says that the object of his criticism was

> something more comprehensive.... It was nothing less than the secular religion of democracy, the "substitute religion" which for more than half a century had been making headway among liberal intellectuals as the Religion of Humanity.[7]

White also says of Stephen that "in the course of a life of sixty-five years he had moved a long way from the Evangelical faith into which he was born."[8] But attenuated though Stephen's religious faith had become, he saw clearly the practical implications of the dechristianization of Western culture, implications whose full import is only dawning on most of us today.

Stephen regarded belief in a personal God and in an afterlife as the religious doctrines of greatest practical importance for society. He wrote:

Upon [these questions] hang all religion, all morals, all politics, all legislation—everything which interests men as men. Is there or not a God and a future state? Is this world all?[9]

Should we ever become convinced that human life ends absolutely in death, Stephen felt,

.... there will be an end of what is commonly called religion, and it will be necessary to reconstruct morals from end to end.[10]

He explained the reason why in these terms

If these beliefs are mere dreams, life is a very much poorer and pettier thing; men are beings of much less importance; trouble, danger, and physical pain are much greater evils, and the prudence of virtue is much more questionable than has hitherto been supposed to be the case. If men follow the advice so often pressed upon them, to cease to think of these subjects otherwise than as insoluble riddles, all the existing conceptions of morality will have to be changed, all social tendencies will be weakened. Merely personal inclinations will be greatly strengthened.[11]

General acceptance of a purely secular view of life, he says,

.... would have an equally powerful and direct influence both on law and morals. The value which is set upon human life, especially upon the lives of the sick, the wretched, and superfluous children would at once appear to be exaggerated. Lawyers would have occasion to reconsider the law of murder, and especially the law of infanticide.[12]

This brings us to where we are now—a century after Stephen wrote. He himself said:

The questions which I have in mind will not arise at all until the great change in religious belief, of which we now witness the beginning, has gone much further and assumed a much more decided character than can be expected, say, for a generation to come.[13]

The process has taken longer than a generation, and is of course even yet not complete. But society in the West, and certainly in English-speaking countries, is now sufficiently dechristianized and secularized that Stephen's predictions are visibly coming true.

What we are getting at, of course, is the inevitability of some form of public morality, whether it reflects traditional values or whether the preferred "morality" is radically individualistic. Typically, the arguments against legal enforcement of traditional moral standards are premised upon the modernist reduction of such questions to the principles of liberty and equality. A liberal society can hardly understand a moral-legal issue other than as a conflict of the rights of autonomous individuals.

There comes a point, however, when such an overwhelming bias in favor of the rights of individuals—and against any conflicting societal or communitarian interests—itself becomes destructive of the very social fabric upon which it depends. We have reached and passed that point. Today the challenge is to overcome the tendency to think of public controversies only in terms of the sovereign state and the sovereign individual, and to learn to think of ourselves more as a community of communities. We must also reject the philosophically and sociologically impossible notion that in a pluralistic society the state can and should be neutral on all matters of morality about which there is disagreement among the people, lest the values of some be imposed on others. This notion, a half truth at best, leads to the establishment of the beliefs of the most secularized, materialistic, and hedonistic elements of the population as normative. If we are a plurality of communities, their right to maintain and transmit the community's beliefs and values is at least as important as the right of the individual to live as he pleases.

To move our law and public policy in this more sane and balanced direction, it is necessary to show how far from true neutrality the current penchant for normlessness has taken us. This is certainly the case on the issue of abortion, where the Supreme Court's 1973 fiat has been followed by more spilled blood than in all of the wars in which Americans have participated since the country's founding. The same question will arise in regard to postnatal life when, as seems likely, euthanasia becomes a constitutional issue. According to the *New York Times,* it has already become the subject of "an emotional debate in Britain," occasioned by the publication of a booklet entitled "How to Die with Dignity" that described various methods of suicide. This debate, the *Times* reported, centered on the questions, "Is there a 'right to commit suicide,' as basic as the right to live? And if there is, is it proper to help people kill themselves, either actively or by advising them?"[14]

The issue thus posed is both basic and unavoidable. The person whose life is to be terminated by euthanasia wants to die. He therefore claims the right to end his life, or to have it ended by a doctor, on the premise that the only value of a life is a purely subjective one, and his life is no longer a value to him. The argument against letting him choose death—when all subsidiary and distracting arguments about fully informed consent have been settled—must invoke the principle that human life is a value in itself, an objective human good, that the state exists to protect. Faced with this issue, the U.S. Supreme Court could not pretend to be neutral by finding euthanasia to be included in the constitutional right of privacy, thus making life and death objects of private choice. So to decide would be to come down on one side of the controversy, that side which holds that life has only subjective value.

Similarly, arguments for recognition of the civil rights of homosexuals, to the extent that they are a demand for public acceptance of heterosexuality and homosexuality as separate but equal ways of life, pose an issue to which there is no neutral answer. This is a demand that the public commit itself to a particular view of the nature and function of sex in human life. Faced with this demand, the public and its government cannot take refuge in a specious neutrality by leaving the matter to individual consciences.

To do so would be a public declaration that in the eyes of society and its laws, sexual preferences are merely that—personal and subjective preferences of no objective validity and no public importance. That view may arguably be the correct one, but it is not a neutral refusal to hold any view at all. Nor, if adopted, would it succeed in relegating questions of sexual preference to the purely private domain.

Consider, for example, the case of *Belmont* v. *Belmont*. A divorced and remarried father applied in the New Jersey Superior Court for a change in the custody of his children from his former wife to himself on the ground that she was living in a lesbian relationship deleterious to the welfare of the children. According to the *Family Law Reporter,* the court "found him to be suitable as a custodian in all respects." Nonetheless, it rejected his application and ruled that "the mother is not to be denied custody merely because of her sexual orientation. Her sexual preference and her living arrangement with her lover are only two of the many factors to be examined in determining the best interests of the children . . ."[15] In so ruling, the court committed the State of New Jersey to the proposition that a homosexual union is, or can be, as acceptable a one in which to raise children as is a heterosexual one dignified by matrimony. This is something more than a decision to leave sexual preferences up to individuals. It is a public stand in regard to the institution of the family.

The point is that there is inescapably a public morality—a good one or a bad one—in the sense of some set or other of basic norms, in the light of which the public makes policy decisions. These norms are moral norms to the extent that they include fundamental judgments on what is good or bad for human beings, judgments about what it is permissible or obligatory to do to them or for them. Public morality is a secular morality inasmuch as it aims only at secular goals, at the welfare of men in this world. It is not therefore a secularist morality. When discussing the welfare of human beings in the here and now we are not limited to the vision of man and his good that happens to be held by those who are completely secularized in their outlook on life. Secularism is not the least common denominator of all American beliefs about human welfare. It is but one sectarian view among many, and any American is free to believe that he derives from his religion a richer, fuller, and more truly human image of man. He is also free to use it as a basis for the views he advocates on public policy.

Leo Pfeffer has announced the Triumph of Secular Humanism, which he seems to regard as the resolution of the Issues That Divide.[16] That victory may or may not be a fact; one sometimes has the impression that the battle is not over yet. But if it proves to be the fact, we should at least not delude ourselves about what has happened. It will not be the advent of a truly neutral state but the replacement of one view of man, and the ethic and the legal norms based on it, by another view.[17]

In the meantime, the Issues That Divide will continue to divide our people ever more deeply. The pluralist game will continue to be played, of course, because there is no other game in town. But there is no need for it to keep on being a confidence game in which one side proclaims its cause as neutrality and the other side is gullible enough to believe it. Societies do face moral issues to which they must give moral answers. The answers we arrive at through the political process in our pluralist society are likely to be rather messy, somewhat confused, and certainly less than universally satisfactory ones. Answers nonetheless will be arrived at, and they will have definite effects on our society. We shall play the pluralist game more honestly, perhaps even with better results, if we admit openly what the game is and what stakes we are playing for.

Although the question of how to govern a pluralistic society is unanswerable in abstract and universal terms, certain suggestions can be made. The first is to refuse resolutely to accept the liberal definition of the question in terms of the individual and the state alone. Society is made up of communities on whose moral health society depends. Pluralism does not require that the communities and their moral beliefs be sacrificed to the equality of all individual preferences. The larger and sounder part of society must have the right and the power to determine the moral limits of permissible action. If the larger part is in fact not the sounder part of society, then society will certainly be in peril—but it will not escape the danger by resorting to an unrestrained radical individualism.

To be more specific, public policy may and ought to take the monogamous family as the basic unit of society, and should support and encourage it in its culture-transmitting function. To aid the family in this function, and to support the different religious and cultural communities to which families belong, the educational system ought to become more open and flexible than it now is. We need to rethink the notion that the secularized public school is the rock on which the republic stands. It may have been possible so to conceive of the public school when it was the agent of a dominant Anglo-Saxon Protestant culture. But now those who are concerned to maintain what is left of that culture would do well to think of other and better relationships between the state, the communities, and the schools.

Finally, while it is not and should not be the function of the state to teach religion, it is in the interest of the society which the state governs that religion should be taught. We need consequently to rethink the proposition that religious freedom consists primarily or exclusively in a separation of church and state made as absolute as possible. Political society and the state depend on social forces which they cannot create but can destroy, and among these religion is one of the principal ones. Some relationship between the state and religion more nuanced than neutrality between religion and irreligion is needed, in the interest of society and the state.

Even these rather modest suggestions will go down hard, if they go down at all in the present climate of American public opinion. The alternative, however, is a steady degeneration of pluralism into mere individualism. That is a prospect which even liberals, if they are intelligent, may contemplate with some dismay.

TEN

"World Views" and Public Policy

Carl Horn

"THE COSMOS IS ALL THAT IS or was or ever will be," proclaims Carl Sagan in his popular public television series, *Cosmos*. "It is the universe that made us," he declares, and "we are creatures of the cosmos."[1] Although packaged as "science" and widely viewed in public schools as a part of the science curriculum, Professor Richard A. Baer, Jr., is correct in saying there is more to the series than an effort "to understand nature scientifically and objectively":

> From beginning to end of *Cosmos,* we see Sagan the admirer, the devotee, the worshipper.... "Our ancestors worshipped the sun," we are told, "and they were far from foolish. It makes good sense to revere the sun and the stars, because we are their children."[2]

Having to argue that Carl Sagan's cosmology is not "values neutral" is typical of the philosophical predicament of the contemporary "social conservative." Traditional Judeo-

Christian beliefs and values cannot be reflected in our law or public policy, we are told, because this would "impose morality" and would violate the "separation of Church and State," a fundamental tenet of our "pluralism." Little attention is given to the fact that public school curricula and other public programs challenge traditional religious beliefs and values with increasing boldness. Rather than the alleged values neutrality, what, in fact, lurks behind these challenges is an alternate religious vision for man and society. As John Dewey expressed it in *A Common Faith*: "Here [in the philosophy underlying public education] are all the elements for a religious faith that shall not be confined to sect, class, or race. Such a faith has always been implicitly the common faith of mankind. It remains to make it explicit and militant."[3]

Progressive sex education is a particularly egregious example of libertine ideology in a public program masquerading as "values neutrality." In *The Great Orgasm Robbery*, a Planned Parenthood publication, for example, we—and our teenage children who receive it in the public schools—are counselled that: "Sex is fun, and joyful . . . and it comes in all types and styles, all of which are OK. Do what gives pleasure and enjoy what gives pleasure and ask for what gives pleasure. Don't rob yourself of joy by focusing on old-fashioned ideas about what's 'normal' or 'nice.' Just communicate and enjoy."[4]

Such advice is standard fare for the progressive sex educators and sexologists for whom religious and moral constraints on human sexuality are just so many hang-ups. As Professor Jacqueline Kasun has written in her provocative study of sex education, "It may come as a surprise to . . . parents . . . that the contemporary sex-education movement does not focus on the biological aspects of sex. . . ."[5] Rather than biology, these courses present what might be called a "genital-centered world view," frequently making Freud look mild in comparison. The Burt and Meeks model sex education curriculum, for example, begins with "a mixed bathroom tour in the first grade" and proposes that sex education be mandatory through at least two years of high school. In each grade students are to keep an elaborately organized "notebook on human sexuality," to include information on such enlightening subjects as "the differences between human sexuality and the sexuality of lower animals," and "pages of details regarding the male and female genital response during sex." The latter are distributed by the National Sex Forum, an organization which pursues its mission to undermine traditional moral values with religious zeal.

Consider several of the recommended items for classroom discussion and activities. In one lesson plan, high school students, working in boy-girl pairs on "physiology definition sheets," are asked to define terms such as "foreplay," "erection," and "ejaculation." In another, small co-ed groups are to be employed to list all of the slang words in our rich American vocabulary for penis, vagina, homosexual, and intercourse. Elsewhere, recommended topics for classroom discussion include, in all seriousness, how students "feel" about drawing pictures of sex organs, and whether they are satisfied with the size of their own.

For those recalcitrant youngsters who, in spite of all the aforementioned, and with publicly funded assistance to the contrary, nevertheless have problems getting their adolescent juices flowing (always "responsibly," of course), there is yet hope in the prescribed segment of the sex ed curriculum on masturbation; this segment, in Dr. Kasun's hometown of Arcata, California, includes a "pre-test" and a "post-test" on the subject. The goals for the seventh and eighth grade curriculum in Arcata specify, for example, that "the student will develop an understanding of masturbation, will view films of masturbation, [and] will 'learn the four philosophies of masturbation. . . .'" [For the educationally underprivileged, the four philosophies of masturbation, to be taught "by participating in a class debate," are identified as "traditional, religious, neutral, and radical."][6]

Whatever one thinks of the appropriate scope of public

school sex education courses, or of the educational benefits derived from requiring students to view the *Cosmos* series, it should be clear that neither, in any meaningful sense, is "values neutral." To the contrary, both are filled with value-laden assumptions and statements, including those which contradict and compete with traditional Judeo-Christian beliefs and values concerning the same subjects. Insofar as either fosters a particular moral/ethical perspective of man and society, it can properly be regarded as inculcating, or imposing, upon school children a particular "world view." Nevertheless, when parents, teachers, or even students, have sought to have more traditional beliefs and values represented in this alleged marketplace of ideas, they have often and increasingly been refused on the ground that even this minimal accommodation would offend our "pluralism."

Accepting arguendo that pluralism does, in some sense, describe the current make-up of American society, it remains at the heart of our inquiry to look behind the rhetoric, stereotypes, and assumptions so often attending this term, in search of substance. What are the requirements and the limitations of this pluralism? Whose beliefs and values should be reflected in the law and public policy of our pluralistic society? Where a value judgment is inevitable and there is conflict, whose views should prevail? Political philosopher Francis Canavan has suggested that it is no accident that basic questions such as these are seldom asked or discussed. "It has been the *genius* of the liberal pluralist society *to avoid raising* ... questions of fundamental philosophy as far as possible," writes Professor Canavan, because if philosophical presuppositions are never identified or discussed, they are less likely to encounter effective challenge.[7]

This ability to ignore the ideological conflicts in contemporary Western society appears to be waning, however, and an increasing number of commentators are calling for a rethinking of basic principles. This is an encouraging trend. Professor Canavan, for example, has likened the exclusion of traditional views under the alleged necessities of "neutrality" and "pluralism" to "an effort [on the part of social liberals] to play the pluralist game with a stacked deck."[8] Professor James Hitchcock's analysis of the use to which the concept of pluralism has been put is to the same effect. "Secular society is far less tolerant than it presents itself to be," charges Hitchcock, "and its official ideology of 'pluralism' is to a great extent an illusion. There are official or quasiofficial opinions which are enforced on a whole range of controversial questions, and those who dissent from these do so at their peril."[9]

Of course, there have been those among the guiding lights of modern public education—which has played a leading role in shaping the current pluralistic ethos—who have realized that theirs, far from being value-free, is an essentially *religious* enterprise. John Dewey, a central figure in this ideological struggle, has been mentioned. As John F. Gardner wrote in *Towards a Truly Public Education*: "[There is] nothing in the whole history of schools from earliest times which affords ground for believing that education can be separated from ultimate life values. An experienced teacher knows that a moral, philosophic, and religious orientation guides his every act . . . Schooling always implies ultimate values."[10] Professor Baer concurs. *"Education never takes place in a moral and philosophical vacuum,"* writes Baer. "If the larger questions about human beings and their destiny are not being asked and answered within a predominantly Judeo-Christian framework, they will be addressed within another philosophical or religious framework—but hardly one that is 'neutral.' "[11]

The same is generally true regarding our public ethic, or publicly affirmed values, and this is an essential point to grasp. The question, again and again, is not *whether* values are to be "imposed," but *which*, or better, *whose* values will be reflected in our law and public policy. Will they be the values of individualistic subjectivism and radical ethical relativism— whether postured under the rubric of "freedom of choice" or any other lofty euphemism—or will they be values which call upon the student or the citizen to discern and submit to certain higher and abiding principles? In this regard, it is observed that while we may be a *pluralistic* society, we are not, and never have been, a *radically secular* society,[12] a distinction often lost in the rhetoric bandied about in public debate of controversial issues. Perhaps the most pressing, and certainly the most fundamental question facing public policymakers in the 1980s, then, is: what vision, what world view, will inform, animate—and limit—the *inherently value-laden* decisions with which we as a society are currently faced?

Increasing attention has been focused on the role of the Supreme Court as an arbiter of fundamental societal values, particularly since *Roe* v. *Wade,* the 1973 abortion decision. In the process, as Joseph Sobran has written, "[T]he court's pretensions to be a panel of experts who merely 'interpret' the law with scrupulous objectivity have suffered. . . ."[13] Citing publication of Woodward and Armstrong's *The Brethren,* in which unseemly political infighting among the Justices is chronicled and detailed, and Justice William O. Douglas' posthumous memoirs, in which Douglas "cheerfully confesses that he . . . decided the Constitution's meaning on the basis of his own 'gut reactions,'" Sobran cites Professor Raoul Berger, who until 1976 was the Charles Warren Senior Fellow in American legal history at Harvard: "The people reluctantly accept [the Court's rulings] because they are told that the Constitution requires it. Would they bow to judicial governance if they understood it merely represents the 'gut' reactions of the Justices?"[14]

A review of recent cases and commentary concerning the First Amendment religion clause reveals the extent to which ideology, and not any constitutional imperative, lies at the basis of our recent jurisprudence in this crucial area.[15] As former Solicitor General Erwin N. Griswold put it while still Dean of Harvard Law School, the courts, particularly the federal courts, are often guilty of mistaking our legitimate American constitutional tradition, which he described as "religious toleration," for the "religious sterility" character-istic of what has come to be called the "strict separation" view.[16] The difference is a terribly important one; the former is characterized by benevolence toward religion and religious values, while the latter is actively hostile, seeking to limit or even eliminate any religious influence on our law and public policy. The former is required by our pluralism, indeed, by our Constitution; the latter is an innovation, a graft upon the constitutional tree urged by those whose primary aim appears to be the complete secularization of our public life and institutions.[17]

Dean Griswold's historically accurate, common sense ap-proach to the role of religion in American life was not to prevail, however, at least not for the succeeding two decades, which were to give birth to a radically different interpretation of the First Amendment.[18] In the process the separation of *Church* and State has come to be widely misconstrued as requiring the separation of *religion* and State, or even the separation of *traditional values* and State. In other words, as the *American Bar Association Journal* editorialized in 1948 follow-ing the Supreme Court's then controversial *Everson* and *McCollum* decisions, the basic error, increasingly prevalent, is that "freedom of religion" has been deemed to require or to be synonymous with freedom *from* religion.[19]

While true children of the Enlightenment may exult in such results, unhappy incongruities remain for the committed secularist. The historical record is clearly on the side of those who favor a more integrated role for religion and religiously based values. The Declaration of Independence sets the tone for much of what is to follow, proclaiming it "self-evident" that we "are endowed by [our] Creator with certain unalien-able Rights" and confessing "a firm reliance on the protection of Divine Providence." Moving ahead about fifteen years, the same Congress which drafted and proposed the First Amendment—to which secularists claim such uncompro-mised allegiance—retained the first congressional chaplain,[20] called upon President Washington to proclaim "a day of public thanksgiving and prayer,"[21] and readopted the Northwest Ordinance providing, in part, for schools which would teach "religion, morality, and knowledge."[22]

Nor does one have to look to what must appear like ancient history to many modernists, who gall at the thought of being ruled by "the dead hand of the past,"[23] to find examples of healthy interaction between religion and our public institutions. Our law, although apparently moving in a secularist direction, is still filled with assumptions and provisions with Judeo-Christian foundations. Our national motto remains "In God We Trust," an inscription borne by our currency since 1865. Since the days of Chief Justice John Marshall, the Supreme Court itself has opened each day's deliberations with the words "God save the United States and this Honorable Court," and as recently as 1952 the Court could write that "we are a religious people whose institutions presupposed a Supreme Being."[24] Both the Senate and the House of Representatives continue to employ chaplains to pray and to provide spiritual counsel,[25] and chaplains serve all branches of the military.[26] We still recognize a National Day of Prayer each year, in the tradition of George Washington and most succeeding presidents, school children pledge allegiance to "one nation under God,"[27] and God is praised and declared trustworthy in our national anthem and other "national songs."

Although there may, in fact, be an element of "civil religion" in these examples of public religious expression, as some critics have charged, the limited point here is that neither the historical record nor our current experience support the view that religion, or religiously based values, must be strictly separated from our public institutions or public life. Rather than fidelity to the Constitution, or to American history, such a view is best understood as primarily reflecting, in its essence, the anti-religious bias proceeding from the Enlightenment—a bias which assumes that religion, if it is to be tolerated at all, should be confined to the strictly private sphere of life.[28] This separationist view, a relative newcomer on the American constitutional scene, is more akin to the militant atheism of the East than it is to the more tolerant and integrationist approach of the West. That those holding this view have been so successful in persuading courts, opinion leaders, and the general public that theirs is a "neutral" position, required by our "pluralism" if not by our Constitution, is indicative of the extent to which the *Zeitgeist,* the spirit of the age, is afflicted by this illegitimate and socially harmful doctrine.

A similar critique can and must be brought to the abortion debate, for here it is just as clearly philosophical commitments, and nothing in our constitution, which have essentially guided the Supreme Court and which essentially guides, whether or not they are consciously aware of it, those who approve of its exercise of "raw judicial power" in 1973.[29] Professor John Hart Ely, now Dean of Stanford Law School and one who disclaims any general anti-abortion sentiments, was indeed correct when he wrote that *Roe* v. *Wade* "is not constitutional law and gives almost no sense of an obligation to try to be."[30] Rather than constitutional principle, as President Reagan reminded us in his recent article in *The Human Life Review,* at the heart of the abortion issue is none other than a profound value judgment:

> The real question today is not when human life begins, but, *What is the value of human life?* The abortionist who reassembles the arms and legs of a tiny baby to make sure all its parts have been torn from its mother's body can hardly doubt whether it is a human being. The real question . . . is whether that tiny human life has a God-given right to be protected by the law. . . .[31]

Certain misconceptions surround recent public debate of moral issues, especially abortion, and obscure the fundamental truths which hang in the balance. Three of these misconceptions bear mention here. The first is the idea, particularly widespread among the college educated, that these controversial public issues are best understood as a clash between conservatives who seek "to legislate morality" and progressives or liberals (or "moderates") who seek to defend our traditional commitment to openmindedness and freedom of conscience. This view is what might be called "the enlightened consensus," encouraged *ad nauseam* by the media's simplistic coverage of groups like the Moral Majority. However, as George F. Will has argued, much the opposite is true: it is as a "progressive" (actually radical) assault on established beliefs and values, and a conservative or traditional response to this provocation, that the recent controversies are best understood. As Will argued in the context of the 1980 political debates over abortion and homosexual rights:

> Don't blame evangelicals for inflating abortion as a political issue. The Supreme Court did that by striking down 50 states' laws that expressed community judgments about the issue. Those who opposed those judgments got them overturned by fiat, not democratic persuasion. There were 1.4 million abortions last year, and the forces that made that possible want subsidies for abortions, knowing that when you subsidize something you get more of it. Yet we are told it is the evangelicals who are aggressive about abortion.
>
> Evangelicals did not set out to alter social attitudes about homosexuality. Government has begun teaching, through many measures, that homosexual and heterosexual relations represent only different preferences (or, in the language of the Democratic platform, "orientations") among "lifestyles." Militant homosexuals are responsible for this, and for making a hot political issue of government attempts to inculcate new attitudes.[32]

A second misconception is that because an issue is controversial, or divisive, it should be removed from the political process and left to private judgment. Such, we are told, is required, again, by our pluralism. In other words, if a group of citizens can engender sufficient controversy over some issue or another, claiming and even sincerely believing that their rights to choose X behavior or entertainment is being unduly impinged, it means the government and the laws ought to withdraw themselves as gracefully and quickly as possible. One obvious problem with this assumption is the one-sided result to which it leads. If two points of view are represented in a debate, say, over measures to be taken against child abuse or pornography, with one side advocating public enforcement action and the other advocating nonenforcement or relegation to private judgment, the latter could win the debate simply by generating a sufficiently distracting controversy. This, one soon learns, is not at all hard to do, and is no way to reach well-reasoned policy decisions in any event. Neither has such a fear of controversy characterized our historical approach to disputes over legal or political questions. The anti-slavery movement was so controversial and divisive that we fought our bloodiest war over it, and its twentieth century counterpart, the civil rights movement of the fifties and sixties, caused all manner of civil disorder, political divisiveness, and other social disruptions. Yet who would suggest that truth, justice, or "the moral high ground" meant leaving decisions regarding slavery or racial discrimination up to "freedom of choice?"

Which brings us back to the freedom to choose an abortion, and the third misconception, the assumption that abortion, to the extent that it is not settled by the Constitution, is primarily a *political* issue. It is not. Abortion is primarily a *moral* issue, with incidental and crucial political implications, to be sure, but still primarily a moral issue. In fact, it might be argued that it is because of the over-emphasis on *political* strategies regarding abortion that the political results to date have been so disappointing. It is not being suggested that politics be ignored, of course; in fact, there are some real anti-abortion heroes among our political leaders. But politics are merely reflective of the demands of the people, and no political opposition could possibly stand in the way of what is urgently needed from Christians, Jews, and others committed to the sanctity, the God-givenness, of human life: a united cry that the killing be stopped.

And make no mistake, we *are* talking about killing.[33] Killing which proceeds in the United States at the rate of over 4,000 unborn children a day. And killing which is cold and calculated and often brutal, as is made so painfully clear in Magda Denes' *In Necessity and Sorrow: Life and Death in an Abortion Hospital.*[34] The author, a clinical psychoanalyst who herself had an abortion in the hospital to which she returned for her study, believes that those who perform abortions, and those who have abortions, can better "deal with" their experiences psychologically and emotionally if all the messy details and feelings are brought out into the full light of day. It is hoped that her candid and graphic revelations would have the opposite effect, sweeping away the cliches and the rhetoric, and forcing the reader to face the hard reality of precisely what an abortion is.

A physician who performs saline abortions, for example, describes to Dr. Denes what happens when the salt is injected: "All of a sudden one notice[s] that at the time of the saline infusion there [is] a lot of activity in the uterus. That's not fluid currents. That's obviously the fetus being distressed by swallowing the concentrated salt solution and kicking violently . . . the death trauma." Another physician who performs saline abortions at the hospital, apparently responding positively to Denes' tell-it-all therapy, mentions "another little thing which I've never read about or mentioned to anyone else. But on a number of occasions, with the needle, I have harpooned the fetus. I can feel the fetus move at the end of the needle, just like you have a fish hooked on the line." This distresses the doctor, for whom rhetoric about pluralism, neutrality, or freedom of choice—or even the huge profits their specialty generates—are no comfort at the moment.

"This gives me an unpleasant, unhappy feeling," confesses the doctor, "because I know that the fetus is alive and responding to the needle stab. . . . You know there is something alive in there that you are killing."[35]

Sometimes in the day-to-day life of the abortion hospital what has been referred to as "the dreaded complication" occurs,[36] that is, the baby which the mother and her doctor have attempted to kill is born alive. A 22-year-old hospital "counsellor" related one such account to Dr. Denes: "The only time I thought about abortions in terms of religion was when I saw fetuses and one was born alive [sic]. I saw one of them, in fact, I even felt the heartbeat. I touched it. It looked like a baby, but it was very tiny. It was real cute. Very quiet. In fact, it was starting to die."[37]

Also on the subject of live births following an attempted abortion, Dr. Denes had this exchange with a 27-year-old hospital social worker.

> Social Worker: "There was one week when there were two live births in the same week. And just, you know, there's this baby crying on this floor while all these women are in the process of trying to deal with their feelings about aborting their babies . . ."
>
> Dr. Denes: "How did the mothers react who gave birth to live babies?"
>
> Social Worker: "Well. This one, she didn't talk much. The mother delivered when there was no one there and there was some period when the mother was holding the baby. And it was grabbing on to her."[38]

To write about surgical abortions, Dr. Denes goes to the operating room to observe first hand. (Holtzman is the doctor and Smith his assistant.)

> 'Forceps please.' Mr. Smith slaps into his hand what look like oversized ice-cube tongs. Holtzman pushes it into the

vagina and tugs. He pulls out something, which he slaps on the instrument table. 'There,' he says. 'A leg. You can always tell fetal size best by the extremities; fifteen weeks is right in this case.'

I turn to Mr. Smith. 'What did he say?' 'He pulled a leg off,' Mr. Smith says. 'Right here.' He points to the instrument table, where there is a perfectly formed, slightly bent leg, about three inches long. It consists of a ripped thigh, a knee, a lower leg, a foot, and five toes. I start to shake badly, but otherwise I feel nothing. Total shock is passionless.

'I have the rib cage now,' Holtzman says, as he slams down another piece of the fetus. 'That's one thing you don't want to leave behind....' Raising his voice and looking at the nurse, who stands next to Dr. Berkowits, he says, 'The table is a little bit too high. I am struggling.' The nurse jumps to crank it lower. 'That's better,' Holtzman says, 'There, I've got the head out now. ...'

I look at the instrument table where next to the leg, and next to a mess he calls the rib cage ... there lies a head. It is the smallest human head I have ever seen, but it is unmistakenly part of a person.[39]

This, then, is something of an insider's view of the ugly day-to-day world of abortion, separated from sophist rhetoric with its question for every answer, its emphasis on exceptions to rules but seldom on the rules themselves, and the never ending harping on "hard cases" which constitute only a minuscule percentage of actual abortions being performed in the United States. What is really behind the pro-abortion initiative of the past ten to fifteen years, as anti-abortion commentators have persistently urged,[40] is no less than an attempt to undermine and replace what bioethicist Peter Singer recently characterized as "the obsolete and erroneous notion of the sanctity of all human life."[41] Urging infanticide—killing—of certain handicapped newborns, Singer looks forward to the day when "the religious mumbo-jumbo surrounding the word 'human' has been stripped away" and secular utilitarian ethics can reign unchallenged by such superstitious encumbrances.[42]

It is true, of course, that issues such as abortion, church-state relations, and public sex ethics result in sharp and intense disagreement among those seeking to influence our law and public policy. Edd Doerr and Paul Blanshard, for example, in a 1973 article in *The Humanist* entitled "The Glorious Decision," euphorically celebrated *Roe* v. *Wade,* proposing "a champagne dinner in honor of the . . . Supreme Court."[43] Doer and Blanshard were both affiliated, interestingly enough, with Americans United for Separation of Church and State. In any event, given their secular utilitarian world view, and their characteristic obsession with the alleged "population explosion," the authors' almost childlike enthusiasm over the abortion decision is understandable. On the other hand, the Judeo-Christian perspective on abortion is perhaps best communicated by Mother Teresa, that saintly woman who has spent her life ministering to the dying on the streets of Calcutta, and who describes abortion simply as "the greatest misery of our time."[44]

An increasing number of issues are resulting in similar divergence of public opinion. The homosexual rights movement is another prominent example. According to the National Organization for Women (NOW), the gay rights movement is in the stream of "the great struggles in history [which require] extraordinary efforts by people dedicated to eliminating prejudice, ignorance, and fear." Pledging itself to "actively work for lesbian and gay rights on local, state, and federal levels," NOW may represent "the enlightened consensus" in calling for "legislation prohibiting discrimination on the basis of sexual preference in all areas. . . ."[45] So far, however, this call for "reform" has not found popular support inasmuch as "the vast majority of Americans reject homosexuality as normative, morally acceptable, or worthy of protection by custom or legislation," as Enrique T. Rueda has written.[46]

Nevertheless, the push for an expansion of homosexual rights and influence is intensifying, and continued morally based grass roots opposition can by no means be taken for granted. Examples of the stepped-up presence of homosexual pressure groups are not hard to find.[47] The inability of the Carter Administration's White House Conference on Families to define "family" was largely due to profound differences over whether homosexual living arrangements should be included. As the 1984 presidential election approaches, every major contender for the Democratic nomination is carrying on open and sympathetic dialogue with homosexual interest groups. And, finally, the dispute over the sex education curriculum goes beyond objection to the advocacy of permissive teenage heterosexuality, to the "thorough and sympathetic treatment" given to homosexuality.[48] "We must finish the contemporary sex revolution," one Planned Parenthood article distributed to high school teachers enjoins; "our society must strive to sanction and support various forms of intimacy between members of the same sex."[49]

What, then, are those who fundamentally differ with the cultural revolution of recent decades to do? How are law and policy makers to be held accountable to the will of the people upon which their public authority ultimately depends? And how are the reins of public institutions to be wrested away from those who continually betray grass roots sentiments and guide our social policy in directions at variance with the moral and intellectual foundations of Western civilization itself?

One primary aspect of any public strategy must be to educate, with particular emphasis on educating religious groups and communities more likely to hold or be sympathetic with traditional Judeo-Christian beliefs and values. Whether we are speaking of First Amendment trends, public school curriculum, abortion, government funding of socially destructive groups, or a host of other contemporary issues, it is essential to recognize that most American citizens, however "well educated" they may be, simply do not know the basic facts. This is due, in part, to the dominance of the primary means of communication—the print media and the major television networks—by those who are sympathetic with the designs and effects of the cultural revolution. The result is a wonder of modern communication technology: otherwise traditional people who are immobilized by largely undefined rhetoric and cliches about "legislating morality," "pluralism," "separation of church and state," etc., but who, often without realizing it, have thought very little about these issues for themselves. Thus, a major aspect of any strategy must be communication of the basic facts, without which intelligent and independent-minded conclusions will remain as elusive as ever.

Second, we must begin to think of contemporary issues such as those we have been discussing less as distinct political or social questions, and more as multiple manifestations of world views in fundamental conflict. Simply stated, the conflict is between those who believe that our law and public policy can and should reflect a belief in God, or at least in a higher moral order, and those—including some professed religious believers—who reject any such grounding of our law and public policy as oppressive or unjust to nonbelievers and moral dissenters. The response to this legitimate concern, of course, is that "democratic dissent is also better protected in a public arena that is, in [Peter] Berger's phrase, under a 'sacred canopy.'"[50] In any event, the important point is that until we see the modern "values crisis" in terms of world views in conflict we will continue to attack symptoms or manifestations of the problem, rather than confronting the illicit presuppositions at their root.

Third, wherever possible we should be gathering rather than winnowing; we must strive to avoid allowing parochial or sectarian differences to divide us. As Richard Neuhaus has correctly observed, "[T]he perception of the collapse of the hegemony of the secular Enlightenment is very widespread,"[51] extending across a broad political and philosophical spectrum. Inasmuch as there is broad agreement, including agreement among believing Christians and Jews, that "any cultural reconstruction that could lead to a reconstituted public ethic must be informed by the classic religious traditions,"[52] this breadth is to be protected and preserved wherever possible. The goal here is to identify a core consensus, and then to develop a public strategy in accord with the broad areas of agreement among our respective theological and intellectual traditions. The alternative, which has dominated our recent experience, is to have our respective efforts running parallel or even at cross purposes with one another.

Fourth, there are a number of pressing questions of a more pragmatic or strategic sort which need to be addressed and settled before such a coalition can become a workable reality. What priority should be assigned to the many contemporary issues currently vying for our time and attention? What means can be employed to educate the various publics, religious and otherwise, regarding the current situation? How can the mass media be utilized with a minimum of distortion, taking into account the inevitable loss of subtlety and nuance in the transmission? How can the message be best framed for dissemination among higher educators and other intellectuals, groups dominated by skepticism and cynicism regarding religion and traditional values? Which issues should be litigated, and which should be the subject of legislative initiatives, including efforts to amend the Constitution, and again, in what order of priority?

Further questions must be raised concerning the individuals and groups which might cooperate in such a movement. How are they to be identified and mobilized in a style and manner which would have broad appeal, including appeal to those for whom sophistication is a *sine qua non*? What role should the clergy and overtly religious groups play in the necessary coalition? From where will leadership come in advancing a public strategy of this scope and dimension, and to whom will it be accountable? And finally, what sources of financial support can be identified for such an ambitious undertaking?

The ancient Hebrew scripture, which Christians likewise revere as the inspired Word of God, is explicit in its teaching that any people must have an informing and motivating "vision." "Where there is no vision," teaches one of the Hebrew proverbs, "the people perish."[53] It is to supply this need for a guiding vision that God gave the Torah and, Christians believe, that God further revealed himself in Christ. One great Christian mind of the twentieth century, that of Aleksandr Solzhenitsyn, understands the modern "values crisis" in terms of a break with this high tradition, marked by what he calls "the flaw of a consciousness lacking all divine dimension."[54] His understanding of how the Western vision has changed over time is instructive:

> Imperceptibly, through decades of gradual erosion, the meaning of life in the West has ceased to be seen as anything more lofty than the "pursuit of happiness." ... The concepts of good and evil have been ridiculed for several centuries; banished from common use, they have been replaced by political or class considerations of shortlived value. It has become embarrassing to appeal to eternal concepts. ...[55]

Solzhenitsyn's prognosis is sobering indeed. "Judging by the continuing landslide of concessions made before the eyes of our own generation alone," he warns, "the West is ineluctably slipping toward the abyss. Western societies are losing more and more of their religious essence as they thoughtlessly yield up their younger generation to atheism."[56]

It is not stylish, of course, to speak about the "religious essence" of modern social or political theory, or to speak negatively of "atheism" for that matter, but then it was not stylishness which characterized the prophetic voices of our past, nor is it style or fashion which can be allowed to guide our way in the future. Indeed, theologian Carl F.H. Henry is closer to the mark than many 'a political pundit. "In this transition period when a foundering society seeks new security . . . the West will find that security only by reasserting its heritage of Judeo-Christian revelation. . . . Americans must make a deliberate choice: either to continue their doom-dealing course of godless self-indulgence, or to opt for the . . . renewal wrought by reaffirming divine dependence and purpose."[57]

However sophisticated we become in our arguments or methods, whatever philosophical subtleties we embrace, let us never lose sight of the simple but profound wisdom with which Solzhenitsyn concludes his Templeton address: "To the ill-considered hopes of the last two centuries, which have reduced us to insignificance and brought us to the brink of nuclear and non-nuclear death, we can propose only a determined quest for the warm hand of God, which we have so rashly and self-confidently spurned."[58] May God grant us the intellectual acumen, the purity of heart, the resolution of will, and the sustaining grace to hear and to heed our brother's eminently wise counsel.

Notes

Chapter Four
On Parents, Children, and the Nation-State

1. Theodore Zeldin, *France, 1848-1945, Vol. II: Intellect, Taste and Anxiety* (Oxford: at the Clarendon Press, 1977), p. 983.
2. Paul Johnson, *Modern Times: The World from the Twenties to the Eighties* (New York: Harper & Row, 1983), p. 147.
3. Rainer C. Baum, *The Holocaust and the German Elite: Genocide and National Suicide in Germany, 1871-1945* (Totowa, N.J.: Rowman and Littlefield, 1981), p. 290.
4. Alexis de Tocqueville, *Democracy in America*, vol. 2, ed. J.P. Mayer (Garden City, N.Y.: Doubleday, 1969), pp. 432, 584-603.
5. Walt W. Rostow, "The National Style," in *The American Style: Essays in Value and Performance*, ed. Elting E. Morison (New York: Harper and Brothers, 1958), pp. 246-313.
6. Transcript of remarks made during a hearing on "The Causes and Societal Consequences of Family Breakdown," United States Senate Subcommittee on Family and Human Services, Committee on Labor and Human Resources, Washington, D.C., September 22, 1983.
7. Daniel P. Moynihan, *Maximum Feasible Misunderstanding* (New York: The Free Press, 1969), pp. xi-xii.
8. Quoted in Jean Bethke Elshtain, "Feminism, Family and Community," *Dissent* (Fall 1982), p. 443.
9. Allan Sherman, *The Rape of the A*P*E* (*American *Puritan *Ethic): The Official History of the Sex Revolution, 1945-1973* (Chicago: Playboy Press, 1973), p. 11.
10. Sherman, *The Rape of the A*P*E**, pp. 338, 347-48.
11. For pure expressions of these ideas, see: David B. Van Vleck, *How and Why Not to Have That Baby* (New York: Paul S. Erikson, 1971); Garrett Hardin, *Stalking the Wild Taboo* (Los Altos, Cal.: William Kaufmann, 1973); and Ellen Peck and Judith Senderowitz, editors, *Pronatalism: The Myth of Mom and Apple Pie* (New York: Thomas Y. Crowell, 1974).
12. Kate Millet, *Sexual Politics* (New York: Doubleday, 1970), pp. 54, 159.
13. Germaine Greer, *The Female Eunuch* (New York: McGraw-Hill, 1970, 1971), pp. 317, 320.
14. Laurel Limpus, "Liberation of Women: Sexual Repression and Family," quoted in Elshtain, "Feminism, Family, and Community," p. 443.

15. Quoted in: Mary Morain, "Panel on Population," *The Humanist* (March-April, 1966), p. 51.
16. Richard M. Nixon, "Message to Congress on Population," *New York Times* (April 30, 1972), Section 12, p. 3.
17. *Population Growth and the American Future: The Report of the Commission on Population Growth and the American Future* (Washington, D.C.: U.S. Government Printing Office, 1972).
18. Eugene Steuerle, "The Tax Treatment of Households of Different Size," ed. Rudolf Penner, *Taxing the Family* (Washington, D.C.: American Enterprise Institute, 1983), pp. 73-97.
19. Ray L. Birdwhistell, "The American Family: Some Perspectives," *Psychiatry* (Aug. 1966), pp. 203-12; "The Idealized Model of the American Family," *Social Casework* (April 1970), pp. 195-98.
20. "Changing Families in a Changing Society," Report of Forum 14, White House Conference on Children and Youth, 1970.
21. Jacquelyn J. Knapp, "Some Non-Monogamous Marriage Styles and Related Attitudes and Practices of Marriage Counselors," *The Family Coordinate* (Oct. 1975), pp. 505-14.
22. "Tucker: Hopes for Conference," *Report from the White House Conference on Families* (August 1979), p. 4.
23. Printed paraphrase of Tamara Hareven, "Changing Realities of Family Life," found in *Listening to America's Families: The Report of the White House Conference on Families* (Washington, D.C.: WHCF, 1980), p. 159.
24. See: Daniel Yankelovich, *New Rules* (New York: Bantam Books, 1981-82), p. 4.
25. Alasdair MacIntyre, *After Virtue* (Notre Dame, Ind.: University of Notre Dame Press, 1981), pp. 235-36.
26. On this point, see Julian L. Simon, *The Economics of Population Growth*. (Princeton, N.J.: Princeton University Press, 1977), who concludes: "... The Malthusian propositions are not correct for the vast majority of today's world—just as they were not correct for the Western world Malthus had in mind" (p. 476).
27. Steuerle, "The Tax Treatment of Households of Different Size."
28. Horace Mann, *The Republic and the School: On the Education of Free Men,* ed. Lawrence A. Crevin (New York: Bureau of Publications, Teacher's College of Columbia University, 1975), p. 111.
29. Lucy Patterson, "Department of Education," in *Agenda '83: A Mandate for Leadership Report,* ed. Richard N. Holwill (Washington, D.C.: The Heritage Foundation, 1983), p. 117. Emphasis added.

Chapter Five
Abortion: The Judeo-Christian Imperative

1. Harold M. Schmeck, Jr., "Twin Found Defective in Womb Reported Destroyed in Operation," *New York Times,* June 18, 1981, p. 19.
2. Thomas Kerenyi and Usha Chitkara, "Selective Birth in Twin Pregnancy

with Discordancy for Downs Syndrome," *New England Journal of Medicine,* June 18, 1981, p. 1525.

3. Schmeck, p. 19.
4. M. J. Sobran, "The Abortion Sect," *Human Life Review,* vol. 1, no. 4 (Fall, 1975), p. 107.
5. Malcolm Potts, "A New Ethic for Medicine and Society," *California Medicine,* vol. 113, no. 3, September, 1970. Reprinted in *Human Life Review,* vol. 1, no. 1 (Winter, 1975), pp. 103-104.
6. Robin Marantz Henig, "Saving Babies Before Birth," *New York Times Magazine,* February 28, 1982, p. 20.
7. Potts, "A New Ethic," p. 103.
8. Ibid., p. 103.
9. Ibid., p. 104.
10. Peter Singer, "Sanctity of Life or Quality of Life?" *Pediatrics,* vol. 72, no. 1, July, 1983, p. 128.
11. Ibid., p. 129.
12. *Roe* v. *Wade,* 410 U.S. 113, 153.
13. Ibid., p. 132. Blackmun was quoting from L. Edelstein, *The Hippocratic Oath,* p. 64.
14. Ibid., p. 130.
15. Ibid., p. 159.
16. Ibid., p. 162.
17. Ibid.
18. Ibid., p. 163.
19. Ibid., pp. 164-65.
20. *Doe* v. *Bolton,* 410 U.S. 179, 191-92. Emphasis in original.
21. Ibid., p. 221.
22. Ibid., p. 222.
23. *Roe* v. *Wade,* p. 162.
24. Hearings before the Subcommittee on Separation of Powers of the Committee on the Judiciary, United States Senate, 97th Congress, First Session, on S. 158, Vol. 1; testimony of Dr. Micheline Mathews-Roth, p. 14.
25. Hearings, testimony of Dr. Hymie Gordon, p. 20.
26. Hearings, testimony of Dr. Jerome Lejeune, p. 18.
27. Hearings, testimony of Dr. Hymie Gordon, p. 13.
28. Senator John P. East, Report to the Committee on the Judiciary, U.S. Senate, made by its Subcommittee on Separation of Powers, 97th Congress, First Session, December, 1981, p. 11.
29. Ibid, p. 11.
30. Warren Hern and Billie Corrigan, "What About Us? Staff Reactions to the D & E Procedure," presented at the meeting of the Association of Planned Parenthood Physicians, San Diego, October 26, 1978.
31. *City of Akron* v. *Akron Center for Reproductive Health, Inc.,* Docket 81-746, June 15, 1983.
32. Sadja Goldsmith, Nancy B. Kaltreich and Alan J. Margolis, "Second Trimester Abortion by Dilation and Extraction (D & E): Surgical

Techniques and Psychological Reactions," presented at the meeting of the Association of Planned Parenthood Physicians, Atlanta, October 13-14, 1977, pp. 2-3.

33. Hern and Corrigan, p. 6.
34. Ibid., p. 9.
35. Liz Jeffries and Rick Edmonds, "Abortion: The Dread Complication," *Today,* Philadelphia *Inquirer,* August 2, 1981, p. 18.
36. Ibid., p. 18.
37. C. Everett Koop, "The Right to Live," *Human Life Review,* vol. 1, no. 4 (Fall, 1975), p. 71.
38. Magda Denes, *In Necessity and Sorrow* (New York: Basic Books, 1976), p. 58.
39. Ibid, pp. 60-61.
40. Ibid, p. 69.
41. Mann's account of her abortion was read into the *Congressional Record* by Rep. Chris Smith, *Congressional Record,* vol. 129, H7320-22, September 22, 1983.
42. *The New Republic,* July 2, 1977, pp. 5-6.
43. John Murray, *Redemption Accomplished and Applied* (Grand Rapids, Mich.: Eerdmans, 1955), p. 116.
44. Clement of Alexandria, *Pedagogus,* ii, 10:95-6.
45. *Didache,* ii, 2.
46. Athenagoras, *Legatio pro Christianis,* P.G., vi, 970.
47. John Calvin, *Commentary on Exodus.*
48. John Weemse, *An Exposition of the Moral Law or Ten Commandments of Almightie God* (London: 1632), pp. 84-87.
49. Karl Barth, *Church Dogmatics,* vol. 111, translated by G.W. Bromiley and T.F. Torrance (Edinburgh: T&T Clark), pp. 415ff.
50. Dietrich Bonhoeffer, *Ethics,* translated by Neville Horton Smith (New York: Macmillan, 1955), p. 131.

Chapter Six
Rationalizing Infanticide:
Medical Ethics in the Eighties

1. See James Manney and John C. Blattner, *Death in the Nursery* (Ann Arbor, Mich.: Servant Publications, 1984) and Nat Hentoff, *Village Voice,* December 6, 1983 through January 10, 1984.
2. It is impossible to estimate the incidence of infanticide accurately, but the available evidence suggests that the nontreatment of handicapped newborns is more than an isolated tragedy. In 1984, Surgeon General C. Everett Koop estimated that the government's "Baby Doe Rules" would save as many as 1200 babies a year. Medical authorities on both sides of the dispute over the Doe rules agree that the practice of withholding treatment because of non-medical considerations was becoming accepted practice in medical centers. Manney and Blattner estimated that approximately 82 infants are born each day with the kind of defects that cause newborns to be unwanted. See Manney and

Blattner, Chapter 2, "The Secret Crime."
3. Raymond S. Duff and A.G.M. Campbell, "Moral and Ethical Dilemmas in the Special Care Nursery," *New England Journal of Medicine* 289 (1973), p. 890.
4. Anthony Shaw, et al., "Ethical Issues in Pediatric Surgery: A National Survey of Pediatricians and Pediatric Surgeons," *Pediatrics*, vol. 60, no. 4, Part 2, October 1977, pp. 588-99.
5. I. David Todres et al., "Pediatricians' Attitudes Affecting Decision-Making in Defective Newborns," *Pediatrics* 60 (1977), pp. 197-201; "Treating the Defective Newborn: A Survey of Physicians' Attitudes," *Hastings Center Report*, April 1976, p. 2.
6. John Lorber proposed selecting only certain spina bifida infants for surgery and letting most of them die. See Lorber's articles, "Results of Treatment of Myelomeningocele," *Development: Medical Child Neurology* 13 (1971), pp. 279-303; Early Results of Selective Treatment of Spinal Bifida Cyctica," *British Medical Journal*, vol. 27 (October 1973), pp. 201-204; "Elective Treatment of Myelomeningocele: To Treat or Not to Treat?" *Pediatrics*, vol. 53, no. 3 (March 1974), pp. 307-308.

R.B. Zachary, a colleague of Lorber's, disputed Lorber's contention that physicians could predict a spina bifida infant's level of functioning at birth. He especially protested the practice of sedating babies not chosen for surgery so heavily that they quickly died of starvation. See his article, "Life with Spina Bifida," *British Medical Journal* 2 (1977), pp. 1460-62.

An American authority, C. Everett Koop, reports that only 25 percent of spina bifida infants in Britain survive, and claims that the "British practice" is also followed in the U.S. See his "Ethical and Surgical Considerations in the Care of the Newborn with Congenital Abnormalities," in Dennis J. Horan and Melinda Delahoyde, eds., *Infanticide and the Handicapped Newborn* (Provo, Utah: Brigham Young University Press, 1982), pp. 89-106.

In 1983, a team of physicians in Oklahoma reported that they had allowed twenty-four spina bifida infants to die because they decided their quality of life would be substandard. The fact that the physicians were proud of these results, and that a prestigious medical journal published their report, renewed fears that infanticide had gained a position of respectability in the medical profession. See Richard H. Gross, M.D., et al., "Early Management and Decision Making for the Treatment of Myelomeningocele," *Pediatrics*, vol. 72, no. 4 (October 1983), pp. 450-58.
7. A.R. Jonson, S.J., et al., "Critical Issues in Newborn Intensive Care: A Conference Report and Policy Proposal," *Pediatrics*, vol. 55, no. 6 (June 1975), pp. 756-68.
8. *Federal Register*, vol. 49, no. 8, Thursday, January 12, 1984, p. 1645.
9. Peter Singer, "Sanctity of Life or Quality of Life?" *Pediatrics*, vol. 72, no. 1 (July 1983), pp. 128-29.
10. Glanville Williams, *The Sanctity of Life and the Criminal Law* (New York: Knopf, 1957). Quoted in James T. Burtchaell, *Rachel Weeping*

(Kansas City: Andrews and McMeel, 1982), p. 296.

11. Michael Tooley, "Abortion and Infanticide," *Philosophy and Public Affairs,* vol. 2, no. 1 (1972), pp. 37-65.

12. Tristram Englehardt, "Ethical Issues in Aiding the Death of Small Children," in Marvin Kohl, ed., *Beneficent Euthanasia* (Buffalo: Prometheus Books, 1975), p. 184.

13. Marvin Kohl, "Voluntary Beneficent Euthanasia," in Kohl, ed., p. 135.

14. "A New Medical Ethic," *California Medicine* (September, 1970), pp. 67-68.

15. Tooley, "Abortion and Infanticide."

16. Fletcher, "Indicators of Humanhood," pp. 1-4.

17. Englehardt, p. 185.

18. Hunter C. Leake III, et al., "Active Euthanasia with Parental Consent," *Hastings Center Report* (October 1979), pp. 19-21.

19. Kohl, p. 135.

20. Daniel C. Maguire, "A Catholic View of Mercy Killing," in Kohl, ed., p. 36. See also Maguire's *Death by Choice* (New York: Doubleday, 1974).

21. Joseph Fletcher, "Ethics and Euthanasia," in Dennis J. Horan and David Mall, eds., *Death, Dying, and Euthanasia* (Frederick, Md.: University Publications of America, 1980), p. 301.

22. Kohl, pp. 133, 134.

23. Englehardt, p. 186.

24. Joseph Fletcher, "The 'Right' To Live and the 'Right' To Die," in Kohl, p. 49.

25. Joseph Fletcher, "Indicators of Humanhood: A Tentative Profile of Man, *Hastings Center Report* (November 1972), p. 3.

26. James T. Burtchaell, *Rachel Weeping* (Kansas City: Andrews and McMeel, 1982), p. 312.

27. *Current Opinions of the Judicial Council of the American Medical Association, 1981,* Article 2.10.

28. This quote and those following are from Fr. McCormick's paper, "To Save or Let Die: The Dilemma of Modern Medicine," *Journal of the American Medical Association,* vol. 229, no. 2 (July 8, 1974), pp. 172-76.

29. Richard A. McCormick, "The Quality of Life, the Sanctity of Life," *Hastings Center Report* (February 1978), pp. 30-36.

30. Richard A. McCormick and Lawrence H. Tribe, "Infant Doe: Drawing the Line," *American Medical News* (October 15, 1982).

31. John J. Paris and Richard A. McCormick, "Saving Defective Infants: Options for Life or Death," *America* (April 23, 1983), pp. 313-17.

32. Dennis J. Horan, "Euthanasia as a Form of Medical Management," in Horan and Mall, eds., *Death, Dying, and Euthanasia,* p. 203.

33. McCormick, "To Save or Let Die," pp. 172-73.

34. McCormick, "The Quality of Life, the Sanctity of Life," p. 30.

35. Fletcher, "The 'Right' To Live and the 'Right' To Die," in Kohl, p. 46.

36. Statement of John J. Paris, "Hearings before the Subcommittee on Family and Human Services," p. 87.

37. John J. Paris, "Terminating Treatment for Newborns: A Theological

Perspective," *Law, Medicine and Health Care* (June 1982), pp. 120-24.
38. McCormick, "The Quality of Life, the Sanctity of Life," p. 174.
39. Paul Ramsey, *Ethics at the Edges of Life* (New Haven: Yale University Press, 1978), p. 156.
40. Clement Smith, M.D., quoted in Ramsey, p. 256.
41. See, for example, Fred Lilly, "Defending the Helpless," *National Catholic Register,* August 28, 1983.
42. For a useful discussion of these points see Donald McCarthy and Edward Bayer, eds., *Handbook on Critical Life Issues* (St. Louis: Pope John XXIII Medical-Moral Research and Education Center, 1982), see especially chapter 13, "Decisions About Prolonging Life."

Chapter Seven
Ideological Biases in Today's Theories of Moral Education

1. For scholarly and popular criticism of Values Clarification, see John S. Stewart, "Clarifying Values Clarification: A Critique," *Phi Delta Kappa,* vol. 56, no. 10 (1975); Alan L. Lockwood, "A Critical View of Values Clarification," *Teachers' College Record* 77 (1975), pp. 35-50; Idem, "Values Education and the Right to Privacy," *Journal of Moral Education* 1 (1977), pp. 19-26; Idem, "The Effects of Values Clarification and Moral Development Curricula on School Age Subjects: A Critical Review of Recent Research," *Review of Educational Research* 48 (1978), pp. 325-64; R.A. Baer, Jr., "Values Clarification as Indoctrination," *The Educational Forum* 41 (1977), pp. 155-65; Idem, "A Critique of the Use of Values Clarification in Environmental Education," *The Journal of Environmental Education* 12 (1980), pp. 13-16; Idem, "Parents, Schools, and Values Education," *Wall Street Journal,* April 12, 1982 (Op-Ed); William J. Bennett and Edwin J. Delattre, "Moral Education in the Schools," *The Public Interest* 50 (1979), pp. 6-9; Martin Eger, "The Conflict in Moral Education: An Informal Study," *The Public Interest* (Spring 1981), pp. 62-80; K.M. Gow, *Yes Virginia, There Is a Right and Wrong* (Rexdale, Ontario: John Wiley, 1980); P.C. Vitz, "Values Clarification in the Schools," *New Oxford Review* 48 (1981), pp. 15-20. P.C. Vitz, "Moral Education: A Comparison of Secular and Religious Models," in *Catechetical Instruction and the Catholic Faithful* (Boston: St. Paul Editions, 1982).
2. The two major works on which this review is based are *Values and Teaching* (Columbus, Ohio: Charles E. Merrill, 1966) by Louis E. Raths, Harmin Merrill, and Sidney Simon; and *Values Clarification: A Handbook of Practical Strategies for Teachers and Students,* 2nd ed. (New York: Hart, 1978) by Sidney B. Simon, Leland W. Howe, and Howard Kirschenbaum.
3. For example, Howard Kirschenbaum is director of the Adirondack Mountain Humanistic Education Center. Values Clarification material is also available from the National Humanistic Education Center, 110 Spring Street, Saratoga Springs, New York 12866. Simon is Professor

of Education at the University of Massachusetts; Howe is professor of Education at Temple University.

4. Simon, Howe, and Kirschenbaum, *Values Clarification,* p. 18.
5. Ibid., back cover; see also pp. 18-22 (emphasis in original).
6. Ibid., p. 15.
7. Ibid., p. 16.
8. Ibid., pp. 18-22.
9. Ibid., pp. 18-19.
10. Ibid., p. 19; original from Raths, Merrill, and Sidney, *Values and Teaching.*
11. For example, Simon, Howe, and Kirschenbaum, *Values Clarification,* devote pp. 13-27 to theory and explanation and pp. 30-379 to the exercises, i.e., to Strategy 1 to Strategy 79.
12. Ibid., p. 26: "Are you *proud* of (do you prize or cherish) your position?" (Emphasis in original.)
13. Nicholas Wolterstorff, *Education for Responsible Action* (Grand Rapids: Eerdmans, 1980).
14. For the concept of "selfism" see Paul C. Vitz, *Psychology As Religion: The Cult of Self-Worship* (Grand Rapids: Eerdmans, 1977).
15. Ibid., ch. 3; also Christopher Lasch, *The Culture of Narcissism* (New York: Norton, 1979).
16. From Wolterstorff, *Education for Responsible Action,* pp. 141-42; originally published in Raths, Merrill, and Sidney, *Values and Teaching.*
17. This, again, is the conclusion of the Wolterstorff study, *Education for Responsible Action,* pp. 143-49.
18. Raths, Merrill, and Sydney, *Values and Teaching,* pp. 36-37.
19. Ibid., p. 145.
20. Ibid., pp. 114-15.
21. Simon, Howe, and Kirschenbaum, *Values Clarification.*
22. Ibid., pp. 44-48.
23. Ibid., pp. 49-53.
24. Bennett and Delattre, "Moral Education," p. 84, note 3.
25. Ibid., p. 86.
26. For a cogent discussion of how Values Clarification violates a student's right of privacy, see Lockwood, "Values Education," and Eger, "Conflict in Moral Education."
27. Kohlberg frequently acknowledges his debt to Piaget (see, for example, Lawrence Kohlberg, "Stage and Sequence: Cognitive-Developmental Approach to Socialization" in D. Goslin, ed., *Handbook of Socialization: Theory Research* (New York: Rand McNally, 1969). He is also quite clear about the seminal importance of Dewey's philosophy (see Lawrence Kohlberg, "A Cognitive-Developmental Approach to Moral Education," by Lawrence Kohlberg, *The Humanist,* November/December, 1972, pp. 13-16).
28. The belief that content and structure can be effectively conceptualized and studied as *separate* categories underlies much contemporary thought and deserves a thorough analysis and critique.

29. From Lawrence Kohlberg, "Stages of Moral Development as a Basis for Moral Education," in *Moral Education: Interdisciplinary Approaches* (Toronto: University of Toronto Press, 1971), pp. 86-87.
30. For example, see William Kurtines and Esther Blank Greif, "The Development of Moral Thought: Review and Evaluation of Kohlberg's Approach," *Psychological Bulletin* 81 (1974), pp. 453-70. Their summary is on pp. 468-69. The entire review, however, constitutes a severe criticism of Kohlberg and it is still cogent after ten years.
31. Lockwood, "The Effects of Values Clarification."
32. Howard Munson, "Moral Thinking—Can It Be Taught?" *Psychology Today*, February 1979, p. 57.
33. Lawrence Kohlberg, New Directions for Child Development, 1978, p. 86.
34. Personal communication to author, December 1979.
35. Thomas P. Kalam, "The Myth of Stages and Sequence in Moral and Religious Development" (Ph.D. dissertation, University of Lancaster, United Kingdom, 1981).
36. Howard Munson, "Moral Thinking," p. 51.
37. Ibid., p. 57.
38. E.V. Sullivan, "A Study of Kohlberg's Structural Theory of Moral Development: A Critique of Liberal Social Science Ideology," *Human Development* 20 (1977), pp. 352-76.
39. Robert T. Hogan and Nicholas P. Emler, "The Biases in Contemporary Social Psychology," *Social Research* 45 (1978), pp. 478-534.
40. Howard Munson, "Moral Thinking," p. 51.
41. Michael Levin, *Commentary* 73 (January 1982), pp. 84-86.
42. Kohlberg, *The Humanist* 38 (November/December 1978), pp. 14-15.
43. Lawrence Kohlberg, "The Child as Moral Philosopher," *Readings in Developmental Psychology Today* (Del Mar, Cal.: CRM Books, 1967, 1968, 1970), pp. 111-12.

Chapter Eight
Trends in State Regulation of Religious Schools

1. See, R. Grunberger, *The 12-Year Reich* (New York: Holt, Rinehart, and Winston, 1979), pp. 313-33.
2. Moneypenney and Buckle, *Disraeli*, vol. 2, pp. 62-63. And see generally S. Arons, *Compelling Belief: The Culture of American Schooling* (1983).
3. Certainly not all government educational bodies do. Under a number of federal and state laws, the liberties of private education have been well recognized.
4. Report of National Commission on Excellence in Education, *A Nation at Risk* (1983).
5. *National Assessment of Education Progress* (1982); J.S. Coleman, *High School Achievement: Public, Catholic and Private Schools* (New York: Basic Books, 1982); T.M. Black, *Straight Talk About American Education* (New York: Harcourt Brace Jovanovich, 1982); P. Copperman, *The*

Literacy Hoax (New York: William Morrow, 1978); R.B. Everhart, *The Public School Monopoly* (Cambridge, Mass.: Ballinger Publishing, 1982); R. Flesch, *Why Johnny Still Can't Read* (New York: Harper and Row, 1981); R. Mitchell, *The Graves of Academe* (Boston: Little, Brown, and Co., 1981); C.E. Silberman, *Crisis in the Classroom* (New York: Random House, 1971); F. Armbruster, *Our Children's Crippled Future* (New York: Times Books, 1977); S.L. Blumfeld, *Why America Still Has a Reading Problem* (1975); R. Kirk, *Decadence and Renewal in Higher Learning* (Chicago: Regnery-Gateway, 1978); John I. Goodlad, *A Place Called School* (1983).

6. H.G. Rickover, "Rescue Foundering Education," *New York Times,* Jan. 30, 1983, p. 19E, col. 3.

7. Even so, in many districts good quality is obviously still to be found, and it should be recognized that there are many conscientious public education leaders who are endeavoring to reverse bad trends of the past recent decades.

8. *School District of Aginton Township* v. *Schempp,* 374 U.S. 203, 225 (1963).

9. *Bob Jones University* v. *United States,* 103 S. Ct., 2017 (1983).

10. They have, by the way, substantial racial minority enrollments.

11. *Keyishian* v. *Board of Regents,* 384 U.S. 589, 604 (1967).

12. *Lemon* v. *Kurtzman,* 403 U.S. 602, 616 (1971).

13. *Murdock* v. *Pennsylvania,* 391 U.S. 105 (1943).

14. *State of Ohio* v. *Whisner,* 351 N.E. 2d 750 (1976).

15. It is true that, in a number of cases, the Supreme Court has made broad statements seeming to recognize a power in the states to regulate nonpublic (including religious) schools. See, *e.g., Board of Education* v. *Allen,* 392 U.S. 236 (1968); *Wolman* v. *Walter,* 433 U.S. 229 (1977). These statements were plainly dicta; none of those cases had involved a situation in which a governmental body was attempting to regulate a school.

16. *Sherbert* v. *Verner,* 374 U.S. 398, 406 (1963).

17. *Lemon* v. *Kurtzman,* 403 U.S. 615.

Chapter Nine
Pluralism and the Limits of Neutrality

1. Alexander Hamilton, John Jay, and James Madison, *The Federalist* (New York: Modern Library), p. 58.

2. Robert A. Dahl, *A Preface to Democratic Theory* (Chicago and London: University of Chicago Press), 1956, p. 45.

3. Ibid., p. 32.

4. Robert Dahl, *After the Revolution?* (New Haven and London: Yale University Press, 1970), p. 25.

5. J.S. Mill, *On Liberty* (New York: Bobbs-Merrill, Library of Liberal Arts, 1956), pp. 112-13.

6. *Reynolds* v. *United States,* 98 U.S. 145, 166 (1878), citing Lieber, "The

Mormons: Shall Utah Be Admitted into the Union?" *Putnam's Monthly,* March 1855, p. 225.

7. James Fitzjames Stephen, *Liberty, Equality and Fraternity,* foreword by R.J. White (Cambridge University Press, 1967), p. 1.

8. Ibid., p. 17.

9. Ibid., p. 101.

10. Ibid., p. 39.

11. Ibid., p. 98.

12. Ibid., p. 48.

13. Ibid., p. 97.

14. Borders, "Suicide Guide Stirs a Debate in Britain," *New York Times,* Sept. 28, 1980.

15. *Belmont* v. *Belmont,* 6 FLR 2785-86 (N.J. Sup. 1980).

16. Leo Pfeffer, "Issues That Divide: The Triumph of Secular Humanism," *Journal of Church and State* 19 (1977), p. 203.

17. For a cold-bloodedly realistic assessment of what will be involved in this shift of views, see the editorial entitled, "A New Ethic for Medicine and Society," *California Medicine* 113 (1970), p. 67.

Chapter Ten
"World Views" and Public Policy

1. Quoted in Richard A. Baer, Jr., " 'Cosmos,' Cosmologies, and the Public Schools," *This World* (Spring/Summer 1983), p. 8. As Professor Baer points out, the overwhelming majority of Americans (82 percent according to an August, 1982, *New York Times* poll) continue to believe that God guided the origin and development of man and 44 percent reject any kind of evolutionary theory whatever. The problem of separating scientific fact from scientific theory, and both from philosophical commitments, is far more difficult than is commonly supposed. At any rate, as Baer observes, it is "small wonder that many object to the teaching of evolution [in public schools], especially when evolution is taught as the cornerstone of a religious-philosophical *world view* rather than as scientific theory." Ibid., p. 5 (emphasis added).

2. Ibid., p. 8.

3. Ibid., p. 14.

4. Rocky Mountain Planned Parenthood, Denver, Colorado, p. 15 (inside back cover). For an informative article about the views on sex advocated by Planned Parenthood, see Addie Jurs, " 'Planned Parenthood' Advocates Permissive Sex," *Christianity Today* (Sept. 3, 1982). The following excerpts are representative: "Losing virginity [is] 'viewed as a move from childhood to adulthood' and a step toward 'independence.' . . . According to our culture . . . marriage should be an 'intimate' and 'lasting relationship,' [but this is a] 'misleading and confining message.' " Instead of buying into this "old fashioned . . . pseudo-submission . . . [characterized by a] geisha mentality," Planned Parenthood's answer is to encourage young people to "explore intimate relationships in

addition to marriage ... [rejecting] the 'old mythology' of saving sex for marriage."

In spite of numerous and repeated efforts to the contrary, Planned Parenthood continues to receive many millions of dollars in public funds each year and is allowed to advocate their views in public schools and other public programs, both domestically and internationally through the U.S. population planning program conducted under the auspices of the Agency for International Development (AID). Those who find Planned Parenthood's views on sex, abortion, sterilization, and related issues unacceptable should make it a priority to press for the denial of public funding and public access to this and like-minded population control and pro-abortion groups.

5. Jacqueline Kasun, "Turning Children Into Sex Experts," *The Public Interest* (Spring 1979). All of the quoted references in this and the following paragraph are from Professor Kasun's article.

6. Ibid. As Professor Kasun puts it: "The objectionable feature of the programs now being promoted by Planned Parenthood, the public health establishment, and other members of the sex lobby is not that they teach sex, but that they do it so badly, replacing good biological instruction with 10 to 12 years of compulsory 'consciousness raising' and psychosexual therapy, and using the public schools to advance their own peculiar *world view.* " Ibid., p. 14 (emphasis added).

7. Francis Canavan, S.J., "The Pluralist Game," *The Human Life Review* (Summer 1983), p. 49 (emphasis added). This article initially appeared in *Duke Journal of Contemporary Problems,* vol. 44, as part of a symposium on these and related issues.

8. Ibid.

9. Peter Williamson and Kevin Perrotta, eds., *Christianity Confronts Modernity* (Ann Arbor: Servant Books, 1981), p. 100.

10. Quoted in James J. Higgins, C.SS.R., *Public Schools and Moral Values* (Liguori, Mo.: Liguori Publications), p. 5.

11. Baer, "Cosmos," p. 15 (emphasis in original). For a thoughtful essay on how a typical high school literature course might "collectively ... deliver the message that the faith preserved in traditional churches no longer connects with the real world" and "create in the teenager the notion that their world divides into the closed religious mind and the open secularist mind," see Frank Zepezauer, "Secular Saints," *The Human Life Review* (Spring 1983), pp. 78, 85. The author, a high school English teacher and an author of a number of high school English textbooks, concludes: "With regard to choices about religion, we should at least want our high school graduates to recognize that they now face two competing ontologies, one affirming a god-centered universe, the other denying it; that men of good will and surpassing intelligence have embraced [both, and] the choice is finally between one *world view* and another. . . ." Ibid., p. 86 (emphasis added). Indeed, our current enthusiasm for "truth in labelling" and "truth in advertising" would seem to require no less.

12. A Gallup poll conducted during the last week of July, 1983, for example,

found what George Gallup, Jr., described as "a rising tide of interest and involvement in religion among all levels of society...." (*Washington Post,* September 14, 1983). According to a *Washington Post* account, "six out of ten Americans said they were currently more interested in religious and spiritual matters than they were five years ago" and "college graduates tended to be as much involved in [religious] activities as those with less education." (Ibid.) See also *The Connecticut Mutual Life Report on American Values in the 80's: The Impact of Belief* (Connecticut Mutual Life Insurance Company, 1981); and George Gallup, Jr., and David Poling, *The Search for America's Faith* (Nashville: Abingdon Press, 1980), for further relevant polling data confirming the substantial religious and moral convictions still held by a substantial majority of the American public. In fact, a *Time* magazine poll of May 1981 suggests that Americans oppose the secularizing influences to which they have been exposed, with seventy-one percent agreeing that "the Supreme Court and Congress have gone too far in keeping religious and moral values out of our lives" and sixty percent expressing the view that "the media reflect a permissive and immoral set of values."

13. Joseph Sobran, "Abuses of Power by the Courts," Los Angeles Times Syndicate, reprinted in *The Seattle Times,* December 8, 1980. Sobran was commenting on *Stone* v. *Graham,* 499 U.S. 39 (1980), in which the Supreme Court ruled that the State of Kentucky had acted unconstitutionally in requiring that the Ten Commandments be posted in its public schools. "In doing so," wrote Sobran, "the court once more imposed its secularist predilections, falsely, in the name of the constitution."

14. Ibid. For a recent study of how judicial predilections have been converted into binding public policy pronouncements through activist court decisions, see Raoul Berger, *Government by Judiciary* (Cambridge, Mass.: Harvard University Press, 1977).

15. See, e.g., Erwin N. Griswold, "Absolute Is in the Dark—A Discussion of the Approach of the Supreme Court to Constitutional Questions," *Utah Law Review* 8 (1963), p. 167; Edward Corwin, "The Supreme Court as a National School Board," *Law and Contemporary Problems* 14 (1949), p. 3 (in which Professor Corwin argued that the Supreme Court was attempting to "remake history" through innovative interpretation of the First Amendment); and authorities cited therein. For more recent discussions of this subject, see Harold Berman, "The Interaction of Law and Religion" *Humanities in Society* (Spring 1979); Carl Horn, III, "Taking God to Court," *Christianity Today* (Jan. 2, 1981); James Hitchcock, "Church, State and Moral Values: The Limits of American Pluralism," *Duke Journal of Law and Contemporary Problems* 44 (1981), p. 1; and Terry Eastland, "In Defense of Religious America," *Commentary* (June 1981).

16. Griswold, "Absolute Is in the Dark," note 15. As Dean Griswold further queried and argued:

> Does our deep-seated tolerance of all religions—or, to some extent of no religion—require that we give up all religious observance in

public activities? It certainly never occurred to the Founders that it would. It is hardly likely that it was accidental that these questions did not even come before the Court in the first hundred and fifty years of our constitutional history. . . . [The religion clauses of the First Amendment] are great provisions, of great sweep and importance. But to say that they require all trace of religion be kept out of any sort of public activity is sheer invention." Ibid., p. 174.

17. See Frank J. Sorauf, *The Wall of Separation* (Princeton, N.J.: Princeton University Press, 1976) for a case-by-case account of the litigating activity of three groups espousing "strict separation"—the American Civil Liberties Union, the American Jewish Congress, and Americans United for Separation of Church and State—during "several decades of increasingly feverish litigation." Specific cases were chosen in an overall agenda intended to dismantle "the American religious establishment," according to Professor Sorauf.

18. Ibid. As Sorauf writes, "Church and state come very late to the U.S. Supreme Court. The entire body of major precedents in the area contains only two [cases] decided before 1951, and both of them were decided in the 1940's. . . ." Ibid., pp. 9-10. Inasmuch as the Amendment these cases purport to interpret was adopted over 150 years earlier (on December 15, 1791), the recency of the Court's current interpretation of its requirements is particularly noteworthy. It is also increasingly controversial, even among the Justices themselves. The internal conflict was conceded in *Walz* v. *Tax Commission,* 397 U.S. 664, 668-69 (1970), for example, where the Supreme Court acknowledged "internal inconsistency in the opinions of the court" construing the Religion Clauses. This inconsistency, wrote Chief Justice Burger, "derives from what, in retrospect, may have been too sweeping utterances on aspects of these clauses which seemed clear in relation to particular cases but have limited meaning as general principles." Justice Burger proceeded to discuss the parameters of what was actually required, or proscribed, by the First Amendment, and then wrote in summary: "Short of those expressly proscribed governmental acts there is *room for play in the joints* productive of *benevolent neutrality* which will permit religious exercise to exist without sponsorship and without interference" (emphasis added). For all the questions it leaves unanswered, "benevolent neutrality" toward religion remains one of the most accurate judicial descriptions of what the First Amendment requires. In short, separation of church and state does not mean, or require, separation of *religion* and state, and state-required silence about religion does not constitute neutrality toward religion.

19. *American Bar Association Journal* 34, pp. 482, 484. The decisions referred to in the text are *Everson* v. *Board of Education,* 330 U.S. 1 (1947) (holding for the first time that the Establishment Clause of the First Amendment applies to the states, and therefore to local schools and communities); and *McCollum* v. *Board of Education,* 333 U.S. 203 (1948) (holding unconstitutional a "released time" religious education pro-

gram held on public school campuses). These decisions lay the legal and philosophical foundation for an increasingly absolutist demand in some quarters for "strict separation" of religion from public life and institutions. Even then, the constitutional and historical analysis of the strict separationists was harshly criticized by commentators. "Undoubtedly the Court has the right to make history," wrote Professor Edward Corwin, "but it does not have the right to *remake* it." Corwin, "The Supreme Court as a National School Board," pp. 3, 20 (emphasis in original).

20. The practice of retaining a chaplain to pray for legislative deliberations was recently upheld by the Supreme Court in *Marsh* v. *Chambers*, 51 U.S.L.W. 5162 (July 5, 1983). "In light of the unambiguous and unbroken history of more than 200 years," wrote Chief Justice Burger for the majority, "there can be no doubt that the practice of opening legislative sessions with prayer has become a part of the fabric of our society. To invoke Divine guidance on a public body entrusted with making laws is . . . simply a tolerable acknowledgement of beliefs widely held by the people of this country." Ibid., p. 5164. A similar historical approach might be taken regarding other public religious expression, including prayer in our public schools. On the latter point, see, e.g., L. Pfeffer, *Church, State and Freedom*, (1953), pp. 394-99; Note "Religion and the Public Schools," *Vanderbilt Law Review* 20 (1967), p. 1078; and *Abington School District* v. *Schempp*, 374 U.S. 203, 277 nn: 53 & 53 (1963) (Brennan, J., concurring) (citing cases and source materials). Finally, in regard to the matter of legislative chaplains, it is noted that the House of Representatives responded to a recent challenge to this practice by reaffirming its commitment to retain a chaplain to pray and provide spiritual counsel by a 388-0 vote. *Congressional Record* 126 (daily ed., Mar. 30, 1982), pp. H1168-73.

21. Quoted in Charles E. Rice, "The Prayer Amendment: A Justification," *South Carolina Law Review* 24 (1972), pp. 705, 715. Nearly every President since Washington has continued this tradition. See Stokes, *Church and State in the United States* (Westport, Ct.: Greenwood Press, 1950), vol. 3, pp. 180-93. In 1952, Congress directed the President to proclaim a National Day of Prayer, 36 U.S.C. 169, an occasion which has been observed with varying degrees of ceremoniousness and piety ever since.

22. Act of Aug. 7, 1789, 1 Stat., 50, 51-52 n. (a), amending and continuing in effect the Northwest Ordinance of 1787. The original Act read in pertinent part: "Religion, morality, and knowledge, being necessary to good government and the happiness of mankind, schools and the means of education shall forever be encouraged."

23. Quoted in Berger, *Government by Judiciary*, note 12, p. 314. This preference to be governed by a "living Constitution" rather than "the dead hand of the past," argues Professor Berger, often results, in practice, in a tendency "to thrust aside the Constitution [by giving] new meanings . . . to the words employed by the Framers . . . reduc[ing] the

Constitution to an empty shell into which each shifting judicial majority pours its own preferences," Ibid., pp. 314-15. The effect is the "continuing revision of the Constitution under the guise of interpretation," allowing the Supreme Court to serve as a *de facto* "continuing constitutional convention." In the process, argues Berger, the meaning of the Constitution is distorted, even lost, and its fundamental prescription for a "rule of law rather than men," is wholly undermined. Ibid., pp. 1-10; 407-18.

24. *Zorach* v. *Clausen,* 343 U.S. 306, 313 (1952). The Court's statement in *Zorach* was simply one example of the long tradition of judicial acknowledgement of our religious heritage. The cases are replete with other examples. See, e.g., *Church of the Holy Trinity* v. *United States,* 143 U.S. 457, 465 (1892), in which the Court said:

> No purpose of action against religion can be imputed to any legislation, state or national, because this is a religious people. This is historically true. From the discovery of this continent to the present hour, there is a single voice making this affirmation.

25. See note 18 above.
26. Similar arguments are made for and against the constitutionality of legislative and military chaplaincy programs. The recent Supreme Court decision upholding the Nebraska Legislature's chaplaincy program, *Marsh* v. *Chambers,* 51 U.S.L.W. 5162 (1983), is likely to insulate the military chaplaincy programs from effective attack as well.
27. 36 U.S.C. 172. For the House of Representatives Report, see H.R. Report No. 1963, 83rd Cong., 2d Sess. (1954). According to the Report, the inclusion of "under God" in the Pledge of Allegiance was intended "to recognize the guidance of God in our national affairs." This, the Report made clear, was not understood to threaten or undermine the "separation of church and state" envisioned by the First Amendment.
28. Theodore M. Kerrine and Richard John Neuhaus, in "Mediating Structures: A Paradigm for Democratic Pluralism" in *The Annals of Political and Social Science* (Nov. 1979, p. 12), put it this way:

> The view that the public sphere is synonymous with the state has been especially effective in excluding religion from considerations of public policy. Two assumptions in modern social thought, deriving from secular Enlightenment traditions, have operated to minimize the role of religion. The first assumption is that religion will inevitably decline in the face of processes of education and modernization. The second is that, even if religion continues to thrive, it deals purely with the private sphere of life and is therefore irrelevant, if not hostile, to public policy.

As the authors argue, "both assumptions need to be reexamined." *Ibid.* Mr. Neuhaus' subsequent writing reflects a certain optimism that we may be entering a period when public policy deliberations will be more accessible to those with explicitly religious views. See, e.g, his "Moral Leadership in Post Secular America," Hillsdale College, 1982 (distributed by the Catholic League for Religious and Civil Rights, Milwaukee, Wisconsin), and his "Who, Now, will Shape the Meaning of America?" *Christianity Today* (Mar. 19, 1982).

29. "Raw judicial power" was the way Justice White characterized the majority opinion in *Roe* v. *Wade,* 410 U.S. 113 (1973) (White, J., dissenting).

30. John Hart Ely, "The Wages of Crying Wolf: A Comment on *Roe* v. *Wade,* " *Yale Law Journal* 32 (1973), pp. 920, 947.

31. Ronald Reagan, "Abortion and the Conscience of the Nation," *The Human Life Review* (Spring 1983), p. 9 (emphasis in original).

32. "Who Put Morality In Politics?" *Newsweek* (Sept. 15, 1980), p. 108.

33. Characterizing abortion as a morally neutral medical procedure was an early strategy of the pro-abortion movement. "Since the old [Judeo-Christian] ethic has not yet been fully displaced," stated an often quoted editorial in *California Medicine* (vol. 113, no. 3, Sept. 1970), "it has been necessary to separate the idea of abortion from the idea of killing." Although conceding that killing "continues to be socially abhorrent" and that "[t]he reverence for each and every life has ... been a keystone of Western medicine," the editorial recognized and welcomed a "new ethic" which it was confident had already substantially undermined and which would ultimately supplant this Judeo-Christian ethic. Describing the strategic ploy to portray abortion as other than killing as "a curious avoidance of ... scientific fact" and "semantic gymnastics," the editorial looked ahead approvingly to a time when "relative rather than absolute valued [would be placed] on ... human lives," and then "birth control and birth selection [would inevitably be] extended to death control and death selection."

34. M. Denes, *In Necessity and Sorrow: Life and Death in an Abortion Hospital* (New York: Basic Books, 1976).

35. Ibid. Quoted in Thomas Ashcraft, "Abortion Hospital: The Staff Feels Guilt and Fear," *The Charlotte Observer* (Jan. 15, 1977).

36. For a gripping account of "the dreaded complication," see Liz Jeffries and Rick Edmonds, "Abortion: The Dreaded Complication," *The Inquirer Magazine* (Aug. 2, 1981), p. 14.

37. Quoted in Ashcraft, "Abortion Hospital."

38. Ibid.

39. Ibid.

40. A fertile and stimulating source of incisive anti-abortion opinion is *The Human Life Review,* published by The Human Life Foundation, 150 East 35th Street, New York, N.Y. 10016. For a succinct and moving comparison of the "sanctity of life ethic" and what has come to be called the "quality of life ethic" see *Abortion: The Silent Holocaust,* by John Powell, S.J. (Allen, Tex.: Argus Communications, 1981).

41. Peter Singer, "Sanctity of Life or Quality of Life?" *Pediatrics* (July, 1983), p. 129. Singer explained what he meant as follows:

We can no longer base our ethics on the idea that humans are a special form of creation, made in the image of God. Our better understanding of our own nature has bridged the gulf that was once thought to lie between ourselves and other species. . . . Once the religious mumbo-jumbo surrounding the term "human" has been stripped away, we . . . will not regard as sacrosanct the life of each and every member of our species. . . . If we compare a severely defective human infant with a nonhuman animal, a dog or a pig, for example, we will often find the nonhuman to have superior capacities for . . . anything . . . that can plausibly be considered morally significant.

42. Ibid. For discussion of infanticide and related issues from medical, legal, and philosophical perspectives, see Dennis J. Horan and Melinda Delahoyde, eds., *Infanticide and The Handicapped Newborn* (Provo, Utah: Brigham Young University Press, 1982); Paul Ramsey, *Ethics at the Edge of Life* (New Haven: Yale University Press, 1978), especially pp. 189-267; and Dennis J. Horan and David Mall, eds., *Death, Dying, and Euthanasia* (Frederick, Md.: Aletheia Books, 1980), especially pp. 75-278.

43. Edd Doerr and Paul Blanshard, "The Glorious Decision," *The Humanist* (May/June, 1973), p. 5.

44. Quoted in Reagan, "Abortion and the Conscience of the Nation," p. 8.

45. "Lesbian Rights: A Woman's Issue; A Feminist Issue; A NOW Issue" (National Organization for Women, Inc., brochure revised Sept., 1982). The areas specifically itemized for legislative reform include "employment, housing, public welfare, health services, *child custody rights*, and immigration and naturalization" (emphasis added).

46. Enrique T. Rueda, *The Homosexual Network* (Old Greenwich, Ct.: Devin Adair, 1982), p. xvii.

47. Rueda, in *The Homosexual Network*, painstakingly documents the recent push toward acceptance of homosexuality as a legitimate lifestyle in the United States. The author examines the homosexual subculture, and then moves on to discuss the goals of the homosexual movement, the various political, intellectual, and religious networks which support it, and its very significant sources of funding. The result is a book which is "must reading" for anyone who seeks to bring traditional values to bear in this troubled area.

48. Kasun, "Turning Children into Sex Experts."

49. Ibid.

50. Personal letter from Richard John Neuhaus to the author, dated November 23, 1982.

51. Ibid.

52. Ibid.

53. Proverbs 29:18 (King James Version). Two more recent versions, The New American Standard Bible and The New International Version, translate the latter phrase "the people are unrestrained" and "the people cast off restraint," respectively.

54. Aleksandr Solzhenitsyn, "Men Have Forgotten God," reprinted in *National Review* (July 22, 1983), p. 872. This address was originally given in London on May 10, 1983, on the occasion of Solzhenitsyn's receipt of the prestigious Templeton Prize in Religion.
55. Ibid.
56. Ibid.
57. Carl F.H. Henry, "The Modern Flight from the Family," in *Emblem of Freedom,* ed. Carl A. Anderson and William J. Gribbin (Durham, N.C.: Carolina Academic Press, 1981), pp. 55, 60.
58. Solzhenitsyn, "Men Have Forgotten God," p. 876.